*"Jerusalem shall be trodden down
of the Gentiles until the times
of the Gentiles be fulfilled"* (Luke 21:24).
It is only during this first week of
June, 1967, that the old city of Jerusalem, to
which Jesus is here referring, has come into the
hands of the Jews who are an independent
nation, Israel. This is the first time Jerusalem
has been in the hands of an independent Israel
since 597 B.C.

Israeli/Arab Conflict

...and the BIBLE

Israeli/Arab
Conflict
...and the BIBLE

BY WILBUR M. SMITH

G/L
REGAL
BOOKS
™

A Division of G/L Publications
Glendale, California, U.S.A.

Second printing, 1968

© Copyright 1967 by G/L Publications
Printed in U.S.A.

Published by
Regal Books Division, G/L Publications
Glendale, California, U.S.A.

Library of Congress Catalog Card No. 67-29634

He-ve-nu sha-lom a-

lei-chem he-ve-nu sha-lom a-

lei-chem he-ve-nu sha- lom a-

lei-chem he-ve-nu sha-lom sha-lom

1: volta   2: volta

sha-lom a-lei-chem sha-lom a-lei-chem

Contents

Preface

In early May, 1967, I was sitting on the spacious veranda of the beautiful Galie Kinnereth Hotel on the western shore of the Sea of Galilee in the city of Tiberias. An Israeli was sitting there, too. He pointed toward the Syrian skies and said, "That's where Israel and Syrian planes were in combat recently." As soon as he spoke I remembered reading about it in the paper. But it seemed to be just another incident between two nations that have known little peace over the centuries. The Bible made reference to a time of peace between them, probably because peace was so scarce. "And they continued three years without war between Syria and Israel" (I Kings 22:1). I sat there reflecting upon the calm of the lake rather than on the strife in the skies.

But in a few short days the calm became chaos. Sabre rattling started; war grew nearer.

"Egypt is mobilizing troops in the Sinai Peninsula."

"Nasser has requested the United Nations to remove its peace-keeping force from the Gaza Strip."

"The Gulf of Aqaba is closed to all shipping."

"Nasser and Hussein have met and reached an agreement. Egyptian officers are now in command of the Jordanian army."

Then, abruptly on June 5th the word was flashed: "War in the Middle East!" The next day: "The old city of Jerusalem has been taken by the Israeli army." In less than a week it was all over and the small land of Israel—about the size of New Jersey—was the focal point of world attention.

But is it all over?

The Christians believe that the events of these recent days are a part of God's plan of the ages. "For Zion's sake will I not hold my peace . . . I have set watchmen upon thy walls, O Jerusalem, which shall never hold their peace night nor day: Ye that make mention of the Lord keep not silent and give him no rest until he make Jerusalem a praise on the earth." (Isaiah 62:1,6)

In the economy of God Jerusalem is the important city of the world. The chief city is not London, nor Paris, nor Washington, nor Moscow. Jerusalem is the city of the great King. It is God's capitol, and the Lord says, "Do not forget Jerusalem until he make Jerusalem a praise on the earth."

In recent years interest in prophetic truth of Scriptures has been dormant, knowledge has been obscured. Suddenly all this has changed. Christians are asking, "What does all this mean? What's next?" Dr. Wilbur M. Smith is one who can help us in our search for answers today. We are grateful for the brilliant scholarship of the choice servants of God. They are men who have not vacillated in their convictions and have not followed the theological trends of the day. They have remained steadfast in their defense and proclamation of God's Word. Dr. Wilbur M. Smith has been a student of Biblical prophetic truth for more than thirty years. He is intimately acquainted with the Middle East from his many visits there and special archeological, historical and Biblical studies.

It was a great privilege in 1966 to have Dr. Smith lead our first GLINT Bible Lands Tour. GLINT (Gospel Literature in National Tongues) participates in Bible study translation programs in more than thirty-five languages. Dr. Smith's lectures in the Bible Lands gave fresh relevancy to the Scriptures, challenges for practical Christian living and insight into God's plan for the unfolding of prophetic truth.

I can think of no one today better qualified to guide us in our consideration of current events in the light of the Bible and particularly the significance of the Israeli-Arab conflict. This book will help you understand the problem a little better and to see the hand of God in the affairs of men. We trust that this small but rich volume will be of inestimable blessing to you in your pursuit of a faith that works today, and until our blessed Lord comes for his own.

CYRUS N. NELSON,
President of GLINT

July, 1967
Glendale, Calif.

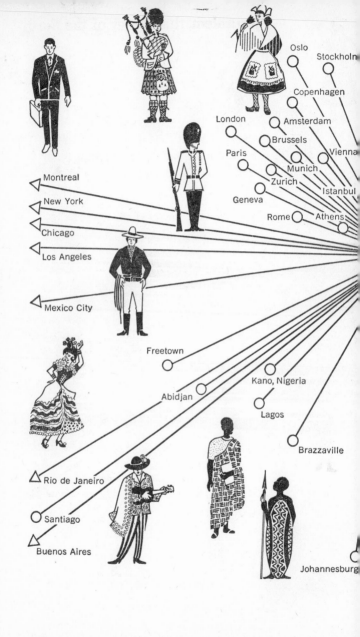

Oslo

Stockholm

Copenhagen

Amsterdam

London

Brussels

Vienna

Paris

Munich

Zurich

Geneva

Istanbul

Montreal

Rome

Athens

New York

Chicago

Los Angeles

Mexico City

Freetown

Kano, Nigeria

Abidjan

Lagos

Brazzaville

Rio de Janeiro

Santiago

Buenos Aires

Johannesburg

Jerusalem, the Center of the Earth

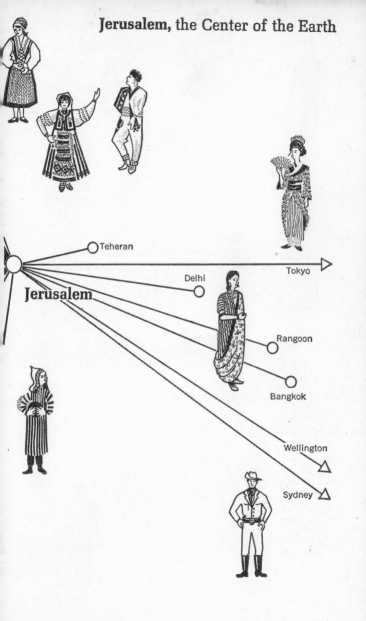

SOME BIBLICAL PASSAGES RELATING TO EVENTS TO OCCUR IN PALESTINE TOWARD THE END

Arranged by Dr. Wilbur M. Smith

I

SOME NAMES AND PROMISES OF THE LAND.

What came to be called Palestine and then the land of Israel is significantly referred to as "the Lord's land" (Hosea 9:3); "the land of promise" (Hebrews 11:9); and called by God Himself "my land" (2 Chronicles 7:20; Jeremiah 2:7; 16:18 etc.); or "Zion of the Holy One of Israel" (Isaiah 60:14). Scores of times in the Old Testament is this land referred to as being *given* by God to Israel and often the text states that it was to be theirs forever (Genesis 13:15; 17:8; Deuteronomy 4:40; Isaiah 60:21).

II

PROPHECIES PREDICTING A FINAL RETURN OF THE JEWS TO PALESTINE, Deuteronomy 4:27-30; Isaiah 11:11,12; Jeremiah 24:6; Ezekiel 32:37-41; 37:21-28.

It is generally agreed there will be an initial return to Palestine resulting from the ambitions

of the Zionists and the unconverted Jews themselves—that they will be brought back, as it were,
in a state of unbelief is probably hinted at in
such a passage as "I will gather you in my anger"
(Ezekiel 22:17; also 36:24-28; 39:25-29).

III

THE AMAZING PROPHECY OF CHRIST CONCERNING JERUSALEM IN THE OLIVET DISCOURSE IN LUKE'S ACCOUNT OF OUR LORD'S GREAT PROPHETIC DISCOURSE.

Here we have a sentence of the greatest relevancy for this hour, "Jerusalem shall be trodden
down of the Gentiles until the times of the Gentiles be fulfilled" (Luke 21:24). It is only during
this first week of June, 1967, that the old city of
Jerusalem to which Jesus is here referring has
come into the hands of the Jews who are an independent nation, Israel. This is the first time
Jerusalem has been in the hands of an independent Israel since 597 B.C.

IV

THE PERPETUAL HATRED OF EDOM.

Edom is identical with Mt. Seir and refers to
those people today called Arabs, descendants of
Esau. The conflict between Esau and Jacob goes
back to Genesis 25:27-34. It appears again in

such passages as Exodus 15:1,16; Numbers 20:14-21; and particularly from a prophetic viewpoint, in Psalm 83; Ezekiel 35:1-12; and the book of Obadiah.

V

THE TIME OF JACOB'S TROUBLE.

That there is still a period when Israel will undergo great suffering, is clear from Jeremiah 30:5-11, etc., and especially Ezekiel 37 and 38, in the events of which Russia will play a large part.

VI

SOME FUTURE EVENTS TO OCCUR IN ISRAEL.

1. The ministry of the two witnesses, Revelation 11:3-12.

2. The erection of a temple in which the man of sin will set himself up as God, 2 Thessalonians 2:4. The name Jerusalem is not in this passage, but no other city can be thought of in this relationship.

3. Peace will ultimately be given to Jerusalem by God through the Prince of Peace, the Son of David (Isaiah 32:18; 33:12-17; 66:12; Ezekiel 34:25 and 37:26).

4. Through this city, and because of the peace to be established, their God will then give peace to the nations of the earth (Haggai 2:9; Zecha-

riah 9:10).

5. Ultimately the nations of the earth will come up to Jerusalem of their own free will for the blessing of God in a great world-wide spiritual revival as in Isaiah 2:1-4; Jeremiah 3:17; 16:19,21; Zechariah 8:20-23 and 14:16-21. Today many of the nations of the Near East think of Jerusalem with hatred, accompanied with a desire to destroy it. Some day they will look to that city for the blessing and the law of the Lord. This will be when Messiah has come to His own people.

This is the time when Psalm 122:6-8 should be our continual experience.

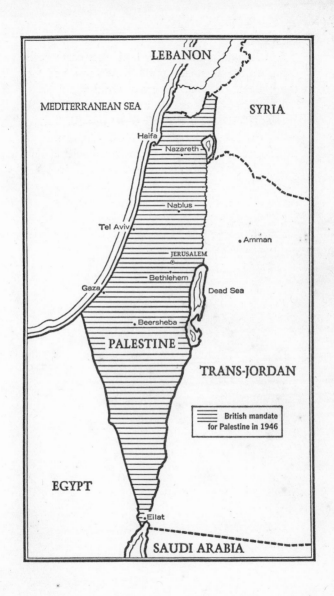

LEBANON

MEDITERRANEAN SEA

SYRIA

Haifa
• Nazareth

• Nablus

Tel Aviv

⊙ JERUSALEM

• Bethlehem

Gaza

Dead Sea

• Amman

• Beersheba

PALESTINE

TRANS-JORDAN

≡≡≡ British mandate
for Palestine in 1946

EGYPT

• Eilat

SAUDI ARABIA

Mid East Crisis and the Bible | **1**

"Behold, he that keepeth Israel
shall neither slumber nor sleep."

Psalm 121:4

More than at any other time in history, because of television and because of other marvels of communication in our age, more millions of people have had their attention focused on Palestine and the lands of the Bible since Monday morning, June 5, of the year 1967 than at any time in world history. Even during the First World War, and the Second World War, though Palestine was involved in those vast struggles, she was not the only battle ground where nations were attempting to decide their destiny; and, of course, in neither of those wars, nor at any time in modern history previous to 1948, had there been a sovereign nation in that land by the name of Israel.

Hour after hour, day and night, in the reports of correspondents and radio and television newscasters, we continually heard of and often looked upon, the very sites identified with such names as the Jordan River, Jericho, Gaza, Bethlehem, Hebron, Nablus, Galilee, and especially Jerusalem, and then within a few hours Sinai, the Gulf of Aqaba, Egypt, Lebanon, Syria. It is within most of these areas that the principal events recorded in our divine revelation took place.

The Bible, in which these names are mentioned hundreds of times, is acknowledged everywhere as a book containing prophecy. All Bible students, Jews and Christians, and indeed many who do not belong to either of these faiths, naturally ask questions at such a time as this. Do these prophetic Scriptures throw any light on this present convulsive crisis? Do they give us anything definite as to what we may yet expect?

I am not approaching this subject as something new for my own research and consideration. I have been reading books on prophetic matters and have been doing some writing on them for something over thirty years. I trust that nothing that I have ever written in the past, or even said from a professor's desk, or from a pulpit, was found to be erroneous or ridiculous in succeeding years. I have studiously avoided the temptation to be sensational, or to make unfounded guesses.

There has always been a marked difference of opinion in the Christian church regarding many of the problems which this crisis raises. Indeed, among many reformed theologians, and many others also, there is the strange conviction that there really is no future for the Jew as a nation on this earth. For many years the idea that the Jews would ever repossess Palestine was ridiculed. Since 1948 the attitude has changed by such to one of condemnation, affirming that the state of Israel is all a mistake on the part of the Jews.

As the references will indicate however, Christian scholars of many preceding generations have supported the view that I have here set forth. I have a deep persuasion that the views we hold are true to the Holy Scriptures, yet we recognize that there is always a possibility of our misunderstanding some of the more intricate details of God's future plans.

I have not thought it necessary in a study such as this to introduce the subject of the Millennium. I do recognize, however, that according to certain passages which will be quoted in this study, some of the conditions that will ultimately prevail in Palestine will only be fully realized during the Millennium.

Neither have I introduced with any fulness at all the pre-eminently important subject of the second advent of Christ. Yet I realize that it will be when he returns, and not before, that the earth will know a permanent peace and a reign of universal righteousness as a reality. I have tried, as far as possible, to focus attention on those prophetic events which relate to Palestine and Jerusalem and have chosen to stress those events which may be occurring within a very short period of time. I am not attempting then to attach to this single subject of the crisis in the Mid East and the prophecies regarding the Holy Land a complete system of eschatology. (If a second edition of this study should be called for, I would hope to add a brief chapter on the future invasion of Palestine as recorded in Ezekiel 38 and 39.)

Ancient Promises to Israel About the Holy Land | 2

"As the mountains are round about Jerusalem, so the Lord is round about his people from henceforth even forever."

Psalm 125:2

Over and over again we have heard the statement that Palestine is "Israel's inalienable possession."

The only adequate ground for such a statement as this would be the Holy Scriptures. And in the ancient covenant of God with Abraham, Isaac, and Jacob, this perpetuity of possession is certainly embraced. "Get thee ... unto a land that I will shew thee," God said to Abraham (Genesis 12:1). Abraham arrived in the Promised Land and God said, "Unto thy seed will I give this land" (Genesis 12:7). Then, a third time, God spoke to Abraham about the land, "Lift up thine eyes, and look from the place where thou art northward, and southward, and eastward, and westward: for all the land which thou seest, to thee will I give it, and to thy seed for ever" (Genesis 13:14,15). Some years later, "I will give unto thee, and to thy seed after thee, the land wherein thou art a stranger, all the land of Canaan, for an everlasting possession; and I will be their God" (Genesis 17:8).

Leupold has tried to avoid the plain meaning of such a promise by translating "to thee will I give it and to thy seed for a long time." He then adds, "This expression actually implies nothing more than an indefinitely long season whose end cannot yet be determined." But then he admits, "Under circumstances the expression may mean actual eternity." He then quotes Luther and Calvin, with whom he agrees, that "this promise to Abraham is conditional requiring faith." Then he makes a statement for which he has no justification, "When the Jews definitely cast off Christ they were definitely as a nation expelled from the land."[1]

The promise of the possession of the land is hinted at again in Deuteronomy 12:1: "These are the statutes and judgments, which ye shall observe to do in the land, which the Lord God of thy fathers giveth thee to possess it, all the days that ye live upon the earth." But it is most emphatically re-stated centuries later in the utterances of Jeremiah, e.g., "Then will I cause you to dwell in this place, in the land that I gave to your fathers, for ever and ever" (7:7). This statement is repeated in the great 25th chapter of this book, "In the land that the Lord hath given unto you and to your fathers for ever and ever" (25:5).[2]

All of the prophecies in the Old Testament regarding Israel's return to the land at the end of this age testify to the truth we have here been emphasizing—a subject that will be discussed in the next chapter.

It seems to me that the very titles which are divinely assigned to this land of Israel imply that ultimately they must be fulfilled. Jehovah Himself calls Palestine "my land": "Then will I pluck them up by the roots out of my land which I have given them; and this house, which I have sanctified for my name, will I cast out of my sight, and will make it to be a proverb and a byword among all nations" (II Chronicles 7:20). He makes a similar assertion in passages from Jeremiah and Ezekiel. "And I brought you into a plentiful country, to eat the fruit thereof and the goodness thereof; but when ye entered, ye defiled my land and made mine heritage an abomination" (Jeremiah 2:7). "And first I will recompense their iniquity and their sin double; because they have defiled my land, they have filled mine inheritance with the carcasses of their detestable and abominable things" (Jeremiah 16:18). "Therefore thus saith the Lord God; Surely in the fire of my jealousy have I spoken against the residue of the heathen, and against all Idumea, which have appointed my land into their possession with the joy of all their heart, with despiteful minds, to cast it out for a prey" (Ezekiel 36:5). "And thou shalt come up against my people of Israel, as a cloud to cover the land; it shall be in the latter days, and I will bring thee against my land, that the heathen may know me, when I shall be sanctified in thee, O Gog, before their eyes" (Ezekiel 38:16). This thought is echoed by Hosea when he refers to it as "the Lord's land": "They shall not dwell in the Lord's land; but Ephraim shall return to Egypt, and they shall eat unclean things in Assyria" (Hosea 9:3). Jerusalem is itself designated by Jehovah as "my city": "I have raised him up in righteousness, and I will direct all his ways: he shall build my city, and he shall let go my captives, not for price nor reward, saith the Lord of hosts" (Isaiah 45:13). Only in the New Testament, strange to say, do we have the famous title, "the land of promise": "By faith he sojourned in the land of promise, as in a strange country, dwelling in tabernacles with Isaac and Jacob, the heirs with him of the same promise" (Hebrews 11:9). For the Jews to be permanently kept out of this land, for Israel to have taken from her these promises to Abraham, which were made without condition, would appear to be a defeat for God. The land upon which he has focused his attention and devotion is certainly not to fail in ultimately being what its divinely given titles indicate, what God intended it to be: the homeland of Israel.[3]

Final Return of Israel to the Land of Promise | 3

"Thus saith the Lord Jehovah: ...
I will take you from among the
nations, and gather you out of all the
countries, and will bring you into
your own land."

Ezekiel 36:22,24,A.R.V.

Even a superficial reading of the prophetic writings of the Old Testament would lead one normally to believe that God has promised to finally restore Israel to her land where she will permanently abide, never again to be rooted up. I am fully aware of the fact that many in the Christian church, true evangelicals, believers in the full inspiration of the Scriptures, nevertheless deny that this is what we should conclude the Old Testament teaches and they assign such prophecies in some strange manner to the history of the church, spiritualizing the prophecies, and denying that they are to be taken literally. Some will say, in reading these pages, that I, the writer, belong to a special school of interpretation. Frankly, I do not any more belong to a special school of interpretation than do those who interpret these prophecies spiritually, as it were, depriving them of their plain and literal meaning. I am sure those who do so spiritualize them will admit that when the reformers and their followers in this area attempt to interpret these passages regarding the return of the Jews to Palestine, their interpretations are vague and often contradict one another and continually introduce the church of Christ in their interpretations in spite of the fact that Palestine is no synonym for the church.

Of all the prophecies regarding this return of the Jews to their homeland, we would most profitably, I believe, begin with a statement found early in the book of Isaiah: "They shall not hurt nor destroy in all my holy mountain; for the earth shall be full of the knowledge of Jehovah, as the waters cover the sea.

"And it shall come to pass in that day, that the root of Jesse, that standeth for an ensign of the peoples, unto him shall the nations seek; and his resting-place shall be glorious.

"And it shall come to pass in that day, that the Lord will set his hand again the second time to recover the remnant of his people, that shall remain, from Assyria, and from Egypt, and from Pathros, and from Cush, and from Elam, and from Shinar, and from Hamath, and from the islands of the sea. And he will set up an ensign for the nations, and will assemble the outcasts of Israel, and gather together the dispersed of Judah from the four corners of the earth" (Isaiah 11:9-12,A.R.V.). We should particularly note here the phrase, "the second time." The first time when God brought back His people to this land was, of course, during the return under Ezra and Nehemiah. There has never been a "second" return. Nothing in the history of Israel can be said to fulfill this particular prophecy. Furthermore, when the Lord brought back these exiles from Persia and Babylon they were not gathered "from the four corners of the earth." Here we might insert another similar statement concluding the prophecies of Amos: "And I will bring back the captivity of my people of Israel, and they shall build the waste cities, and inhabit them; and they shall plant vineyards, and drink the wine thereof; they shall also make gardens, and eat the fruit of them. And I will plant them upon their land, and they shall no more be plucked up out of their land which I have given them, saith Jehovah thy God" (Amos 9:14,15, A.R.V.).[1] This prophecy also has not been fulfilled for the Jews returning under Ezra and Nehemiah were, six centuries later, pulled up out of that land and scattered among the nations of the earth. As Isaiah phrases it, "thy people . . . shall inherit the land for ever" (Isaiah 60:20). We should add here, as others have remarked, that the church was never plucked up out of any land and then brought back again to this same unknown land.

It seems to me that there are two different periods in which the Jews will return to Palestine. The first will be the result of their own genius, courage, determination, vision, and hard work. There is nothing wrong with any of these factors, but one cannot actually say that the coming of two million Jews into Palestine since the beginning of this century is part of any great spiritual movement in which the Jews are led by God himself. In fact, it is quite otherwise. Though modern Israel has greatly encouraged the study of the Scriptures, for which we are grateful, and brought new hope to the breast of these fearfully tormented people when millions were being slaughtered under Hitler, it still is not a religious movement. Zionism does not necessarily insist upon religious factors in conjunction with its political fervor. Dr. Theodor Herzl, the founder of the Zionist movement, was not himself a religious man.

Almost all the kibbutzim, the communal agricultural villages in Israel, are without synagogue or temple. A great mass of these Jews have no religious experience at all, and many, of course, do not acknowledge a personal God. It may be to this part of the return that Ezekiel refers in the following passage: "And the word of Jehovah came unto me, saying, Son of man, the house of Israel is become dross unto me: all of them are brass and tin and iron and lead, in the midst of the furnace; they are the dross of silver. Therefore thus saith the Lord Jehovah: Because ye are all become dross, therefore, behold I will gather you into the midst of Jerusalem. As they gather silver and brass and iron and lead and tin into the midst of the furnace, to blow the fire upon it, to melt it; so will I gather you in mine anger and in my wrath, and I will lay you there, and melt you. Yea, I will gather you, and blow upon you in the fire of my wrath, and ye shall be melted in the midst thereof. As silver is melted in the midst of the furnace, so shall ye be melted in the midst thereof; and ye shall know that I, Jehovah have poured out my wrath upon you" (Ezekiel 22:17-22,A.R.V.).[2]

Over and over again, however, there are references in the prophetic writings to a return of the Jews to their homeland which will be created, watched over and consummated by God himself. A good illustration is from this same book of Ezekiel: "Therefore thus saith the Lord Jehovah: Now will I bring back the captivity of Jacob, and have mercy upon the whole house of Israel; and I will be jealous for my holy name. And they shall bear their shame, and all their trespasses whereby they have trespassed against me, when they shall dwell securely in their land, and none shall make them afraid; when I have brought them back from the peoples, and gathered them out of their enemies' lands, and am sanctified in them in the sight of many nations. And they shall know that I am Jehovah their God, in that I caused them to go into captivity among the nations, and have gathered them unto their own land; and I will leave none of them any more there" (Ezekiel 39:25-28,A.R.V.).[3] Notice the sequence here, and "after" they have borne their shame, "when" they are dwelling safely in the land, "then" will they know that the Lord is their God. This same idea is expressed in an earlier chapter when the Lord says that He will take the Jews out from among the nations and bring them into their own land, and then will he sprinkle clean water upon them and then shall they be clean. (See Ezekiel 36:24-25.)

Then is introduced a more important fact, far more important than a mere geographical location. The Israelites will undergo a cleansing experience in their own hearts. The passage is worth quoting: "A new heart also will I give you, and a new spirit will I put within you; and I will take away the stony heart out of your flesh, and I will give you a heart of flesh. And I will put my Spirit within you, and cause you to walk in my statutes, and ye shall dwell in the land that I gave to your fathers; and ye shall be my people, and I will be your God. I will save you from all your uncleannesses: and I will call for the grain, and will multiply the fruit of the tree, and the increase of the field, that ye shall receive no more reproach of famine among the nations" (Ezekiel 36:26-30,A.R.V.).

Ezekiel then went on to explain his vision of "the valley of dry bones" in which the very bones of the Israelites would have life breathed into them: "Therefore prophesy, and say unto them, thus saith the Lord Jehovah: Behold, I will open your graves, and cause you to come up out of your graves, O my people; and I will bring you into the land of Israel. And ye shall know that I am Jehovah, when I have opened your graves, and caused you to come up out of your graves, O my people" (Ezekiel 37:12,13,A.R.V.). And later in this same chapter the prophet interprets "the sign of the two sticks" (one for Israel and the other for Judah) declaring that the Lord would make them "one stick": "Thus saith the Lord Jehovah: Behold, I will take the children of Israel from among the nations, whither they are gone, and will gather them on every side, and bring them into their own land: and I will make them one nation in the land, upon the mountains of Israel; and one king shall be king to them all: and they shall be no more two nations, neither shall they be divided into two kingdoms any more at all: neither shall they defile themselves any more with their idols, nor with their detestable things, nor with any of their transgressions; but I will save them out of all their dwelling-places, wherein they have sinned, and will cleanse them: so shall they be my people, and I will be their God.

"And my servant David shall be king over them; and they all shall have one shepherd: they shall also walk in mine ordinances, and observe my statutes, and do them. And they shall dwell in the land that I have given unto Jacob my serv-

27

ant, wherein your fathers have dwelt; and they shall dwell therein, they, and their children, and their children's children for ever: and David my servant shall be their prince for ever. Moreover I will make a covenant of peace with them; it shall be an everlasting covenant with them; and I will place them, and multiply them, and will set my sanctuary in the midst of them for evermore. My tabernacle also shall be with them: and I will be their God, and they shall be my people. And the nations shall know that I am Jehovah that sanctifieth Israel, when my sanctuary shall be in the midst of them for evermore" (Ezekiel 37:21-28,A.R.V.).

In another place in his prophecy, Ezekiel reiterates the Lord's promise that Israel will be restored to the land of her fathers by the Lord Himself: "Thus saith the Lord Jehovah: I will even gather you from the peoples, and assemble you out of the countries where ye have been scattered, and I will give you the land of Israel. And they shall come thither, and they shall take away all the abominations thereof from thence. And I will give them one heart, and I will put a new spirit within you; and I will take the stony heart out of their flesh, and will give them an heart of flesh; that they may walk in my statutes, and keep mine ordinances, and do them: and they shall be my people, and I will be their God" (Ezekiel 11:17-20,A.R.V.).[4]

Perhaps we should have one word from another prophetic writing, Jeremiah: "For I will set mine eyes upon them for good, and I will bring them again to this land; and I will build them, and not pull them down; and I will plant them, and not pluck them up" (Jeremiah 24:6). One of the greatest of all passages referring to this truth, possibly the finest summary of all, is in the middle of this book of Jeremiah, the book of judgment, and the book of hope: "Behold, I will gather them out of all countries, whither I have driven them in mine anger, and in my wrath, and in great indignation; and I will bring them again unto this place, and I will cause them to dwell safely. And they shall be my people, and I will be their God: and I will give them one heart and one way, that they may fear me for ever, for the good of them, and of their children after them: and I will make an everlasting covenant with them, that I will not turn away from following them, to do them good; but I will put my fear in their hearts, that they may not depart from me. Yea, I will rejoice over them to do them good, and I will plant them in this land assuredly with my whole heart and with my whole soul" (Jeremiah 32:37-41,A.R.V.).[5] As an illustration of how unnaturally the reformers treat these passages, I cannot help introducing Calvin's remarks on the precious promise, "I will cause them to dwell safely." Calvin says, "After having promised to them a return, he promises now a tranquil condition: for it would have been better for the Jews to remain always in exile and in foreign lands, than to return to their own country and to live there in misery. This was the reason why the Prophet expressly added, that there would be a quiet habitation for them.

"But we know that this was not fulfilled when the Jews returned to their own country; for they were greatly harassed by their neighbours, and the building of the Temple was at first hindered, and they endured many troubles from all quarters, and at length they were oppressed with tyranny by the Syrian kings, and reduced to such extremities, that exile would not only have been more tolerable, but even pleasanter and more desirable, in comparison with the many miseries with which they were oppressed. But, as it has been said elsewhere, whenever the Prophets prophesied of the return of the people, they extended what they taught to the whole kingdom of Christ. For liberation from exile was no more than the beginning of God's favour: God began the work of true and real redemption when he restored his people to their own country; but he gave them but a slight taste of his mercy. This prophecy, then, with those which are like it, ought to be extended to the kingdom of Christ."[8]

The following prophecies describe a condition in Israel which has not been obtained since the State of Israel was established in 1948, but which will some day be literally fulfilled. "In his days Judah shall be saved, and Israel shall dwell safely: and this is his name whereby he shall be called, THE LORD OUR

RIGHTEOUSNESS" (Jeremiah 23:6); "Therefore fear thou not, O my servant Jacob, saith the Lord; neither be dismayed, O Israel: for, lo, I will save thee from afar, and thy seed from the land of their captivity; and Jacob shall return, and shall be in rest, and be quiet, and none shall make him afraid" (Jeremiah 30:10); "Behold, I will gather them out of all countries, whither I have driven them in mine anger, and in my fury, and in great wrath; and I will bring them again unto this place, and I will cause them to dwell safely" (Jeremiah 32:27); "In those days shall Judah be saved; and Jerusalem shall dwell safely: and this is the name wherewith she shall be called, The Lord our righteousness" (Jeremiah 33:16); "But fear not thou, O my servant Jacob, and be not dismayed, O Israel: for, behold, I will save thee from afar off, and thy seed from the land of their captivity; and Jacob shall return, and be in rest and at ease, and none shall make him afraid. Fear thou not, O Jacob my servant, saith the Lord: for I am with thee; for I will make a full end of all the nations whither I have driven thee: but I will not make a full end of thee, but correct thee in measure; yet will I not leave thee wholly unpunished" (Jeremiah 46:27, 28); "And they shall dwell safely therein, and shall build houses, and plant vineyards; yea, they shall dwell with confidence, when I have executed judgments upon all those that despise them round about them; and they shall know that I am the Lord their God" (Ezekiel 28:26);

"And the tree of the field shall yield her fruit, and the earth shall yield her increase, and they shall be safe in their land, and shall know that I am the Lord, when I have broken the bands of their yoke, and delivered them out of the hand of those that served themselves of them. And they shall no more be a prey to the heathen, neither shall the beast of the land devour them; but they shall dwell safely, and none shall make them afraid" (Ezekiel 34:27,28); "And thou shalt say, I will go up to the land of unwalled villages; I will go to them that are at rest, that dwell safely, all of them dwelling without walls, and having neither bars nor gates. Therefore, son of man, prophesy and say unto Gog, Thus saith the Lord God; In that day when my people of Israel dwelleth safely, shalt thou not know it?" (Ezekiel 38:11,14); "After that they have borne their shame, and all their trespasses whereby they have trespassed against me, when they dwelt safely in their land, and none made them afraid" (Ezekiel 39:26). When this great migration occurs and by the will and power of God, they are in the land, they will never again be uprooted. (Jeremiah 24:6) "For I will set mine eyes upon them for good, and I will bring them again to this land: and I will build them, and not pull them down; and I will plant them, and not pluck them up." (Amos 9:14, 15) "And I will bring again the captivity of my people of Israel, and they shall build the waste cities, and inhabit them; and they shall plant vineyards, and drink the wine thereof; they shall also make gardens, and eat the fruit of them. And I will plant them upon their land, and they shall no more be pulled up out of their land which I have given them, said the Lord thy God." "Thy people also shall be all righteous: they shall inherit the land for ever, the branch of my planting, the work of my hands, that I may be glorified. A little one shall become a thousand, and a small one a strong nation: I the Lord will hasten it in his time" (Isaiah 60:21,22). "And it shall come to pass, that like as I have watched over them to pluck up, and to break down, and to throw down, and to destroy, and to afflict; so will I watch over them, to build, and to plant, saith the Lord" (Jeremiah 31:28). "Yea, I will rejoice over them to do them good, and I will plant them in this land assuredly with my whole heart and with my whole soul" (Jeremiah 32:41). This idea of God's planting Israel as a nation in Palestine is a figure of speech used sometimes in reference to God's first planting of Israel in the land during the conquest of Joshua and later times. "Yet I had planted thee a noble vine, wholly a right seed: how then art thou turned into the degenerate plant of a strange vine unto me?" (Jeremiah 2:21). "For the Lord of hosts, that planted thee, hath pronounced evil against thee, for the evil of the house of Israel and of the house of Judah, which they have done against themselves to provoke me to anger in offering incense unto Baal" (Jeremiah 11:17).

Between these two periods of migration and settling in the land will occur a time of terror and tragedy for Israel. This is referred to in the very passages which also tell of the great blessedness and prosperity that will ultimately attend Israel's living in the land. Every thing we have been attempting to say here seems to be unfolded in greatest detail in the 30th chapter of the book of Jeremiah. Early in this profound passage we have the general announcement, which though we have mentioned it above, is worth repeating: "For, lo, the days come, saith Jehovah, that I will turn again the captivity of my people Israel and Judah, saith Jehovah; and I will cause them to return to the land that I gave to their fathers, and they shall possess it" (Jeremiah 30:3, A.R.V.). "I have surely heard Ephraim bemoaning himself thus: Thou hast chastised me, and I was chastised, as a bullock unaccustomed to the yoke: turn thou me, and I shall be turned; for thou art the Lord my God" (Jeremiah 30:18). A great statement is found in verse 10 concerning the condition of Israel in this divine movement: "Jacob shall return, and shall be in rest and be quiet and none shall make him afraid." "And I will gather the remnant of my flock out of all countries whither I have driven them, and will bring them again to their folds; and they shall be fruitful and increase. And I will set up shepherds over them which shall feed them: and they shall fear no more, nor be dismayed, neither shall they be lacking, saith the Lord" (Jeremiah

23:3,4). In chapter 30 we have the statement that in that period, Israel will suffer as a woman in travail for "it is even the time of Jacob's trouble; but he shall be saved out of it" (verse 7). This theme is enlarged upon in verse 11: "For I am with thee, saith the Lord, to save thee; though I make a full end of all nations whither I have scattered thee, yet will I not make a full end of thee: but I will correct thee in measure, and will not leave thee altogether unpunished." It is at this time of Jacob's trouble that the prophecy of Zechariah and the invasion of the northern powers will take place: "Behold, the day of the Lord cometh, and thy spoil shall be divided in the midst of thee. For I will gather all nations against Jerusalem to battle; and the city shall be taken, and the houses rifled, and the women ravished; and half of the city shall go forth into captivity, and the residue of the people shall not be cut off from the city. Then shall the Lord go forth, and fight against those nations, as when he fought in the day of battle" (Zechariah 14:1-3). We will speak of this with more detail in a later section of our study.

Then there are some dark days ahead for Israel, but ultimately a time of undisturbed security, a period not only of prosperity but of a greater spiritual blessedness than she has ever yet known.

There is one more theme identified with this return of Israel, which we have kept for the last, and that is, after Israel is in the land and undergoes a great spiritual revival, there will come to rule in her midst none other than "David their king, whom [the Lord] will raise up unto them" (Jeremiah 30:9); "And I will set up one shepherd over them, and he shall feed them, even my servant David; he shall feed them, and he shall be their shepherd" (Ezekiel 34:23); "And say unto them, Thus saith the Lord God; Behold, I will take the children of Israel from among the heathen, whither they be gone, and will gather them on every side, and bring them into their own land: And I will make them one nation in the land upon the mountains of Israel; and one king shall be king to them all: and they shall be no more two nations, neither shall they be divided into two kingdoms any more at all: Neither shall they defile themselves any more with their idols, nor with their detestable things, nor with any of their transgressions; but I will save them out of all their dwellingplaces, where in they have sinned, and will cleanse them: so shall they be my people, and I will be their God. And David my servant shall be king over them; and they all shall have one shepherd: they shall also walk in my judgments, and observe my statutes, and do them" (Ezekiel 37:21-24). This, of course, can be none other than the Son of David, the Lord Jesus himself. "Afterward shall the children of Israel return, and seek the Lord their God, and David their king; and shall fear the Lord and his goodness in the latter days" (Hosea 3:5). Keil has a great statement on this matter: "The true return to the Lord cannot take place without a return to David their king, since God has promised the kingdom to David and his seed forever. This king David, however, is none other than the Messiah . . . The return was not to take place till the end of the days which does not denote the future generally but always the closing future of the kingdom of God, commencing with the coming of the Messiah."

There are four different basic attitudes toward these prophetic announcements concerning the return of Israel to Palestine. One is that these prophecies were all fulfilled in the return of the Jews under Ezra and subsequent decades. This, however, is contradicted by three facts: The Jews that returned under Ezra, and later leaders, did not come from the four quarters of the earth and from all the nations of the earth, but only from Babylon and Persia. Isaiah 11:11 speaks clearly of a return that is designated as a second one, and there has been no second one up to this century. Finally, the passages we have been discussing which predict a return insist that when this takes place, Israel will be planted in the land forever. She was not so planted with the return under Ezra.

Another theory proposed is that God is through with Israel and that in her rejection of Christ she has forfeited all expectations of being specially dealt with by the Lord at any future time. The answer to this is that Israel's apostasy and disobedience are foreseen by the very prophets who also speak of a time to come when Israel will turn from her disobedience and accept her Messiah.

A third theory is that these prophecies are fulfilled in the history of the church. This principle of interpretation is called spiritualizing and leads to a chaotic, confused suggestion as to what these phrases mean when they speak of the land and Jerusalem and agricultural richness, and especially the reign of David their king over Jerusalem. The church is not a body of people originally belonging to God and now being brought back to him, but is made up of lost sinners. They never knew God and are brought out of their spiritual death to newness of life. This newness of life can never be identified with a migration to Palestine.

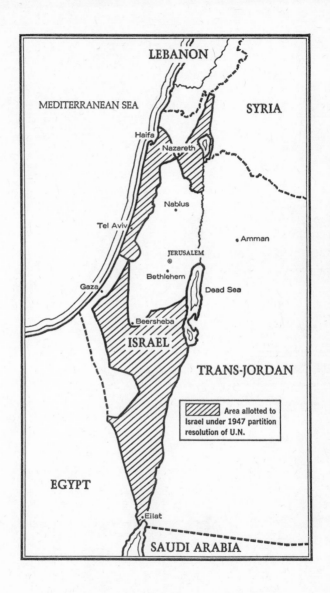

LEBANON

MEDITERRANEAN SEA

SYRIA

Haifa

Nazareth

Nablus

Tel Aviv

Amman

JERUSALEM

Bethlehem

Gaza

Dead Sea

Beersheba

ISRAEL

TRANS-JORDAN

EGYPT

Area allotted to
Israel under 1947 partition
resolution of U.N.

Eilat

SAUDI ARABIA

The Use of These Promises and Their Interpretation | 4

"Lift up now thine eyes, and look from the place where thou art northward, and southward, and eastward, and westward: for all the land which thou seest, to thee will I give it, and to thy seed forever."

Genesis 13:14,15

One could fill an entire book with pages show-ing what the Jews have made of these promises regarding their return to Palestine, but I will here mention only three of them. The historian of Zionism, Dr. Nahum Sokolow quotes a number of passages from the Pentateuch under the head-ing, "The Prophets and the Idea of a National Restoration." In quoting Leviticus 26:32-45 and Genesis 13:14,15, he vigorously declares, "It is impossible to understand how it can be said that this covenant will be remembered, if the Jewish people is to continue dispersed, and is to be for ever excluded from the land here spoken of. As to the return from Babylonian captivity, that will not answer the intention of the covenant at all. For to restore a small part of the Jewish people to its own land for a few generations, and afterwards disperse it among all nations for many times as long, without any hope of return, cannot be the meaning of giving that land to the seed of Abram for ever ... The real Moses, the Moses of the Pentateuch, brands Dispersion as a curse, and his whole religious conception, with all the laws, ceremonies, feasts, etc., is built up on the basis of the covenant with the ancestors, a covenant immovable and unalterable. No matter whether Jews call themselves religious or nationalists: the Jewish religion cannot be separated from nationalism, unless another Bible is invented."[1]

During the hearing of the British Royal Commission on Palestine, Mr. David Ben Gurion, chairman of the Executive of the Jewish Agency for Palestine, declared, "The Bible is our mandate. The mandate of the League is only a recognition of this right and does not establish new things."[2]

On July 9, 1947, in the 24th meeting of the United Nations Special Committee on Palestine (UNSCOP) testimony was heard from Rabbi Fischman, Chief Rabbi of the city of Jerusalem.

Sir Abdur Rahman: "When was the promise made by God?"

Rabbi Fischman: "The promise was given to Abraham, Isaac and Jacob about four thousand years ago."

Sir Rahman: "When was it confirmed by God?"

Rabbi Fischman: "It was reaffirmed to Moses."

Sir Rahman: "Did God also promise that ten tribes would arise out of Ishmael, son of Hagar and Abraham?"

Rabbi Fischman: "He did not. Twelve tribes would arise only out of Jacob, the son of Isaac."

Sir Rahman: "According to the Jews, was not their return to this country to take place with the appearance of the Messiah?"

Rabbi Fischman: "No. In accordance with the Jewish tradition, the Jews should return to Palestine before the Messiah comes, and Jerusalem should be a part of Palestine. Only then, after the return of the Jews of Palestine, in accordance with the tradition, the Messiah will arrive."

Sir Rahman: "How long after the return of the Jews to Palestine will the Messiah arrive, according to you?"

Rabbi Fischman: "This is a thing nobody can tell."[3]

The Interpretation of These Prophecies by Protestant Expositors

Here again we could easily produce an entire book of pages from students of the Scriptures from the Reformation down to today, but here we have space for only a very few references. In 1673 an interesting book was published, with a preface by Dr. John Owen, "A Collection of

47

Prophecies which Concern the Calling of the Jews and the Glory that Shall Be in the Latter Days." The scores of references were classified under eight headings which may be of interest to my readers:

"I. The Jews shall be gathered from all parts of the earth where they now are scattered, and brought home into their own land.

"II. They shall be carried by the Gentiles to their place; who shall join themselves with the Jews, and become the Lord's people.

"III. Great miracles shall be wrought when Israel is restored, as formerly when they were brought out of Egypt—viz.:

1. Drying up the river Euphrates.
2. Causing rivers to flow in desert places.
3. Giving them Prophets.
4. The Lord Christ himself shall appear at the head of them.

"IV. The Jews, being restored, and converted to the faith of Christ, shall be formed into a State, and have Judges and Counsellors over them as formerly: the Lord Christ himself being their King, who shall then also be acknowledged King over all the earth.

"V. They shall have the victory over all their enemies, and all kings and nations of the earth shall submit unto them.

"VI. The Jews, restored, shall live peaceably, without being divided into two nations, or contending with one another any more.

"VII. The land of Judea shall be made eminently fruitful, like a Paradise, or the Garden of God.

"VIII. Jerusalem shall be rebuilt, and after the full restoration of the Jews shall never be destroyed, nor infested with enemies any more." All of this material was quoted by the famous Dr. Philip Doddridge in a work now seldom seen.[4]

A writer who should be of great interest to Americans especially is Increase Mather, who when twenty-five years of age became pastor of the Second Church in Boston. When only forty-two years of age he was elected president of Harvard, an honor he declined. Later when the invitation was extended in 1685 he accepted, and remained as president for sixteen years. By the time he was forty-five he had already published twenty-five volumes. The first of his many works on prophecy was published in London in 1669, entitled "The Mystery of Israel's Salvation Explained and Applied—a discourse concerning the general conversion of the Israelitish nation." Though we do not agree with all of his statements, Mather says, regarding Israel's restoration:

"When once God shall begin this work of Israel's salvation, it shall be carried on with speed and irresistible might ... All motions, when they come near their center, are most swift ... 'The Israelites, at their return, shall even fly' (Isaiah 11:14). Besides, the Lord Jesus is eager in His pursuit, when once He is near unto the possession of His glorious kingdom upon earth ... Christ will do more work, and destroy more adversaries in a few years in the last times than in many years in former days" (Isaiah 60:22).

Concerning the matter of the return of the Jews to their own land, Mather is clear: "Some have believed and asserted a general conversion of the Jews, yet have doubted whether they should ever again possess the land of their fathers. But the Scripture is very clear and full in this, that you see not how it can justly be denied or questioned." "And they shall build the old wastes, they shall raise up the former desolations, and they shall repair the waste cities, the desolations of many generations" (Isaiah 61:4); "For, lo, the days come, saith the Lord, that I will bring again the captivity of my people Israel and Judah, saith the Lord: and I will cause them to return to the land that I gave to their fathers, and they shall possess it" (Jeremiah 30:3); "Thus saith the Lord God: In the day that I shall have cleansed you from all your iniquities I will also cause you to dwell in the cities, and the wastes shall be builded. And the desolate land shall be tilled, whereas it lay desolate in the sight of all that passed by. And they shall say, This land that was desolate is become like the garden of Eden; and the waste and desolate and ruined cities are become fenced, and are inhabited" (Ezekiel 36:33-35); "In that day will I make the governors of Judah like an hearth of fire among the wood, and like a torch of fire in a sheaf; and they shall devour all the people round about, on the right hand and on the left: and Jerusalem shall be inhabited again in her own place, even in Jerusalem" (Zechariah 12:6); "And the Lord shall be king over all the earth: in that day shall there be one Lord, and his name one. All the land shall be turned as a plain from Geba to Rimmon south of Jerusalem: and it shall be lifted up, and inhabited in her place from Benjamin's gate unto the place of the first gate, unto the corner gate, and from the tower of Hananeel unto the king's winepresses. And men shall dwell in it, and there shall be no more utter destruction; but Jerusalem shall be safely inhabited" (Zechariah 14:9-11).

Even the great period of Israel's tribulation was not hidden from Mather's mind. Later in the book he amplifies this truth: "A little before the conversion of the Jews, there will be the most terrible doings in the world that ever were heard of in respect of wars and commotions, the waves of the sea roaring, confused noise, and garments rolled in blood, blood and fire, and vapor of smoke; but after the kingdome shall be restored unto Israel, then shall be glorious days of peace and tranquillity."[5] "And in that day will I make a covenant for them with the beasts of the field, and with the fowls of heaven, and with the creeping things of the ground: and I will break the bow and the sword and the battle out of the earth, and will make them to lie down safely" (Hosea 2:18); "And men shall dwell in it, and there shall be no more utter destruction; but Jerusalem shall be safely inhabited"(Zechariah 14:11); "For thus saith the Lord, Behold, I will extend peace to her like a river, and the glory of the Gentiles like a flowing stream: then shall ye suck, ye shall be borne upon her sides, and be dandled upon her knees" (Isaiah 66:12); "Violence shall no more be heard in thy land, wasting nor destruction within thy borders; but thou shalt call thy walls Salvation, and thy gates Praise" (Isaiah 60:18); "And he shall judge among many people, and rebuke strong nations afar off; and they shall beat their swords into plowshares, and their spears into pruninghooks: nation shall not lift up a sword against nation, neither shall they learn war any more. But they shall sit every man under his vine and under his fig tree; and none shall make them afraid: for the mouth of the Lord of hosts hath spoken it" (Micah 4:3,4).

A notable preacher, both in Great Britain and America, at the beginning of the nineteenth century was Dr. Elhanan Winchester; in 1800 he published a most interesting volume entitled, "A Course of Lectures in the Prophecies that Remain to Be Fulfilled." The third lecture was devoted to the thesis that "The return of the Jews to their own land is certain." In this lecture, Dr. Winchester said: "As the Turkish power has always been a great enemy to the Jews and having their land in possession at this time, nothing can well be more evident then that the Turkish power must be greatly weakened before the Jews can return to their country and possess it ... This event may be easily accomplished if the nations that shall weaken the Turks make this one of their demands, namely, that they which yield up the holy land to its rightful owners, the Jews, to repossess which God sware to give to the patriarchs and their posterity." He even foresaw a great conflict to take place here. "The nations round them will make a general combination against them when they least expect it and will gather a numerous and very formidable host to effect their destruction. In this they shall not finally succeed."[6]

Without quoting any more of the vast literature of the nineteenth century, let me simply call attention to the words of William E. Blackstone, in his famous book, "Jesus Is Coming," "If Israel is beginning to show signs of national life and is actually returning to Palestine, then surely the end of this dispensation is nigh, even at the doors." A remarkable memorial, asking that the United States take action to assist the Jews of the world in obtaining Palestine as their national home was presented to Benjamin Harrison, president of the United States. This petition, signed by a great number of distinguished clergymen, professional men, mayors, and members of Congress, opened with the following paragraph:

"Why not give Palestine back to them again? According to God's distribution of nations it is their home—an inalienable possession from which they were expelled by force. Under their cultivation it was a remarkably fruitful land,

sustaining millions of Israelites, who industrious-
ly tilled its hillsides and valleys. They were
agriculturists and producers, as well as a nation
of great commercial importance—the center of
civilization and religion."[7]

I never tire of quoting a penetrating statement
of this subject of the Jews and Palestine appearing nearly a century ago in a work now seldom
consulted, but still valuable, by the German
scholar, J. H. Kurtz: "As the body is adapted and
destined for the soul, and the soul for the body;
so is Israel for that country and that country for
Israel. Without Israel, the land is like a body
from which the soul has fled; banished from its
country, Israel is like a ghost which cannot find
rest."[8]

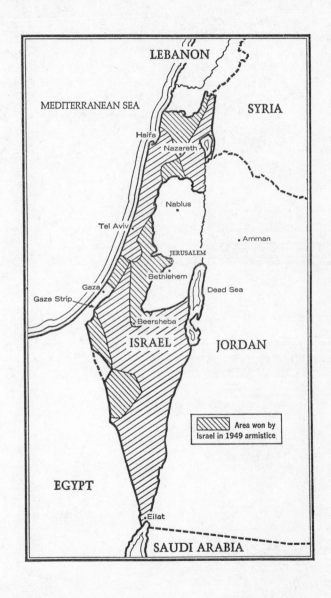

The Creation of Modern Israel | 5

"Then was our mouth filled with laughter, and our tongue with singing: then said they among the nations, Jehovah hath done great things for us, whereof we are glad."

Psalm 126:2

The predictions of Israel's great prophets regarding the ultimate return of their people to Palestine have confronted all Bible students for centuries. I suppose one might say the prophecies have also been held by some Jews as the assurance of a condition of ultimate restoration. But it is only in modern times that there has been a real movement among the Jews to do something definite about this matter of their return, and, of course, it is only since 1948 that at last the world has seen an actual State of Israel established among the nations of the earth. Actually Palestine has never been divorced from the heart-longings of the Jews. This is superbly expressed by no less a person than Dr. Chaim Weizmann, the then President of the Zionist organization and of the Jewish agency for Palestine, in a statement which he made before the Palestine Royal Commission gathered in Jerusalem on November 25, 1936.

"What has produced this particular mentality of the Jews which makes me describe the Jewish race as a sort of disembodied ghost—an entity and yet not an entity in accordance with the usual standards which are applied to define an entity? I believe the main cause which has produced the particular state of Jewry in the world is its attachment to Palestine. We are a stiff-necked people and a people of long memory. We never forget. Whether it is our misfortune or whether it is our good fortune, we have never forgotten Palestine, and this steadfastness, which has preserved the Jew throughout the ages and throughout a career that is almost one long chain of inhuman suffering, is primarily due to some physiological or psychological attachment to Palestine. We have never forgotten it nor given it up. We have survived our Babylonian and Roman conquerors. The Jews put up a fairly severe fight and the Roman Empire, which digested half of the civilized world, did not digest small Judea. And whenever they once got a chance, the slightest chance, there the Jews returned, there they created their literature, their villages, towns, and communities. And, if the Commission would take the trouble to study the post-Roman period of the Jews and the life of the Jews in Palestine, they would find that during the nineteen centuries which have passed since the destruction of Palestine as a Jewish political entity, there was not a single century in which the Jews did not attempt to come back."[1]

SOME EARLIER EXPRESSED DESIRES OF THE JEWS FOR A PERMANENT RESIDENCE IN THE HOLY LAND

Dr. Nahum Solokow, the historian of Zionism, in his very remarkable book, "Hibbath Zion" (The Love for Zion), tells us that even as early as the twelfth century, Abraham Ibn Ezra, "In spite of his progressive and somewhat independent ideas, emphasised the importance of the attachment to Palestine, maintaining that every Jew who possesses any property or share in that land is sure to enjoy the eternal life."[2] (See Genesis 33.)

An American, by the name of Mordecai Manuel Noah (1785-1851), wrote a book that had considerable influence, "Discourse on the Restoration of the Jews" (1844).

To pass by a number of other similar writings we should note that in 1860, there was founded what came to be a most influential institution, the Alliance Israelite Universille in Paris. In the same year, there was held the first conference of Hibbath Zion under the leadership of Rabbi Hirsch Kalischer, who by the way, insisted that sacrifices should be resumed in Israel.

In 1861 in London was established the Society for Colonizing Palestine. At this time also Lord Shaftesbury, the wealthy Christian philanthropist, became interested in this subject. It was just at this time, though in Germany, that Moses Hess (1812-1875) wrote his famous book, "Rome and Jerusalem." He had hoped, but in vain, that it would be France who would aid the Jew in founding colonies in the Palestinian area.

Also at this time Baron Edmund de Rothschild began his remarkably fruitful efforts to establish agricultural colonies in Palestine, some of which proved most profitable. In this period a large number of Protestant Evangelical students of Biblical prophecy began to produce volume after volume regarding the future of the Jews including their restoration to Palestine. Indeed the article on Zionism in the "Encyclopedia Britannica" acknowledges that "the interest in a return of the Jews to Palestine was kept alive in the first part of the nineteenth century, more by Christian millenarians, especially in Great Britain, than by the Jews themselves."[3] What the author means by "millenarians" is simply those who believed and wrote about the second coming of Christ, and a subsequent millennium. I have given a list of some of these volumes written at this time in the appendix to this subject. It must be admitted that the pogroms carried out by Czar Alexander II (1855-1881) as well as the amazing increase of anti-Semitism in Germany compelled many Jews to give serious consideration to this matter of the possibility of relocating these persecuted people in some kind of a colony in Palestine.

THE BEGINNING OF ZIONISM

There now arose most opportunely, providentially almost one would say, one of the great leaders of Judaism of modern times, no less a person than Theodor Herzl, a brilliant Austrian journalist. It was he who called together the first Zionist Congress in Basle, Switzerland, in 1897. Strange to say, Herzl was not a religious man, though, of course, he was not anti-religious. In that first Congress, in all the messages that he brought, and in the resolutions that were passed, there was not a single reference to the God of Abraham, Isaac, or Jacob, or even a single quotation from any of the prophetic writings. Herzl's pamphlet, "The Jewish State," published in February, 1896, swept through the Jewish world like a tornado, or to change the figure of speech, it electrified the Jews. Within a few months, Zionist groups sprang up in Jewish communities everywhere. The following is the resolution passed regarding its goals.

"Zionism strives to create for the Jewish people a home in Palestine secured by public law. The Congress contemplates the following means to the attainment of this end:

1. The promotion on suitable lines of the colonisation of Palestine by Jewish agricultural and

industrial workers.

2. The organisation and bringing together of the whole of Jewry by means of appropriate institutions, local and international, in accordance with the laws of each country.

3. The strengthening and fostering of Jewish national sentiment and consciousness.

4. Preparatory steps towards obtaining Government consent where necessary to the attainment of the aim of Zionism."[4]

In 1903, there was a great deal of discussion about the possibility of locating Jews in a homeland of their own in Uganda, South Africa. This was bitterly opposed by Herzl and by most of the Zionists. They insisted there was only one homeland for the Jew, and that was Palestine. Slowly the Jews began to move into the land of their fathers. By 1914, ninety thousand Jews were living in Palestine with forty-three Jewish agricultural settlements. The leadership of Zionism now passed to Chaim Weizmann, whose great gifts as a chemist notably aided Great Britain in the First World War. He interviewed leaders of almost all modern countries and tirelessly advocated by speeches and writings and organizations this whole movement for the ultimate possession of Palestine.

THE YEAR 1917

Two great events took place in the year 1917, which bore directly upon this Palestinian matter. On November 2, 1917, the famous Balfour Declaration was issued. It is important enough to be quoted in full.

FOREIGN OFFICE
November 2nd, 1917

"Dear Lord Rothschild,

"I have much pleasure in conveying to you, on behalf of His Majesty's Government, the following declaration of sympathy with Jewish Zionist aspirations which has been submitted to and approved by the Cabinet:

"His Majesty's Government view with favour the establishment in Palestine of a national home for the Jewish people, and will use their best endeavours to facilitate the achievement of this object, it being clearly understood that nothing shall be done which may prejudice the civil and religious rights of existing non-Jewish communities in Palestine, or the rights and political status enjoyed by Jews in any other country.

"I would be grateful if you would bring this declaration to the knowledge of the Zionist Federation."

Yours sincerely,

ARTHUR JAMES BALFOUR"[5]

THE BRITISH MANDATE

The Council of the League of Nations approved July 24, 1922, a mandate over Palestine to be held by Great Britain, which was retained until 1947. Winston Churchill, in a statement of June 3, 1947, announced that the Balfour Declaration did not mean "the imposition of a Jewish nationality upon the inhabitants as a whole but the further development of the existing Jewish community with the assistance of Jews of the other parts of the world in order that it may become a center in which the Jewish people as a whole may take on grounds of religion and race an interest and a pride." Many Jews felt that the promise of England in the original Balfour Declaration was here betrayed.

During the time this mandate was held, Great Britain had a troublesome problem on her hands. "From the beginning the Arabs in Palestine bitterly resisted Zionism and the British policy supporting it. Several times they rose in revolt, especially in 1929 and in 1936-39, claiming the right of national self-determination, as they represented the large majority of the inhabitants, and demanding the preservation of Palestine as an Arab homeland. Therein they were supported by all the other Arabs. The British repressed the Arab rising for independence, but recognized the genuine character of Arab nationalism and Arab fears. The British government sent various commissions of inquiry and devised various schemes, culminating in the White Paper of May 17, 1939, to reconcile the irreconcilable demands of the Arab population and Zionism for the control of Palestine."[6]

The other event, which occurred in the year

1917, was of course the capture of Jerusalem by General Allenby, leader of the British forces. The whole of the Christian world, and the Jews also, felt that perhaps this was the beginning of the fulfillment of many prophecies, but they were disappointed. Dr. Abba Hillel Silver, one of the great orators of modern Judaism, declared before the Ad Hoc Committee on Palestine of the United Nations General Assembly, October, 1947: "Jerusalem is the ancient capital of the Jewish nation and the symbol throughout the ages of Jewish nationhood. The undefeated resolve of our people to be reconstituted as a nation in the land of Israel was epitomized in the solemn vow of the psalmist and of the exiled people throughout the ages: 'If I forget thee, O Jerusalem, let my right hand forget her cunning.' We strongly urge that the Jewish section of modern Jerusalem, outside the walls, be included in the Jewish State."

THE JEWISH STATE

In the meantime, the Jewish population of Palestine was growing. By 1935 there were 300,000 Jews in Palestine. In 1936 the Jews actually owned by purchase, 350,000 acres of land, for the most part for agricultural purposes. The British High Commission for Palestine departed May 14, 1948, and on the same day, the Jewish National Council and the General Zionist Council, meeting at Tel Aviv, proclaimed the establishment of a Jewish State to be called Israel. Mr. David Ben Gurion was appointed Prime Minister and two days later, Dr. Chaim Weizmann, was elected President of the Provisional Council. The government of the United States recognized Israel as a nation immediately and Russia soon followed. Israel was accepted by the United Nations, May 11, 1949, by a vote of thirty-seven for and twelve opposed.[7]

The problem of the international status of Jerusalem has never been solved. Up until June, 1967, of course, there were two Jerusalems—on the West that belonging to Israel, actually its capital; and on the East, separated by No Man's Land, the old walled city of Jerusalem, containing the holy places, assigned to the Kingdom of Jordan.

The attempt to internationalize this city has come to nothing, even though it has had the voted approval of the United Nations. The General Assembly of the United Nations toward the end of 1948, soon after the establishment of the State of Israel, decided that Jerusalem was to be internationalized. This decision met with violent opposition from Jews everywhere, though it was supported by an encyclical from Pope Pius XII, issued on April 15, 1949, "In Multiplicibus."

On November 29, 1949, at Lake Success, the Soviet Union demanded that the United Nations General Assembly proceed with the plan for the international administration of the Jerusalem area, which it had adopted two years previously.

A comment on this in the "New York Times" of the following day bears careful study: "The Soviet Union, having been barred from taking part in the United Nations' missions regarding both Palestine and the former Italian colonies, is all the more anxious to have something to say about Jerusalem. The Soviet Union, together with the other great powers, is a permanent member of the Trusteeship Council, and this may explain why it wants the Trusteeship Council to take over the responsibility for drafting a final settlement for Jerusalem."[8]

On December 7, 1949, the Special Political Committee of the United Nations General Assembly made its decision regarding the internationalization of Jerusalem, approving this action by a final vote of 35 to 13, with 11 abstentions. Oddly enough, the strongest opposition to this proposal was led by the United States and Great Britain.

In part, the text of the resolution reads that it is the intention of the General Assembly of the United Nations, "that Jerusalem should be placed under a permanent international regime . . .

(1) That the city of Jerusalem shall be established as a 'corpus separatum' under an international regime and

(2) shall be administered by the United Nations

(3) The city of Jerusalem shall include the present municipality of Jerusalem, plus the sur-

rounding villages and towns, the most southern being Bethlehem, the most western Ein Karem, and the most northern Shufat."[9]

This embraces an area of approximately seventy square miles. One of the foremost authorities on international subjects, Edwin L. James, writing for the "New York Times," began his article on this decision as follows: "The vote by the United Nations Assembly to internationalize the city of Jerusalem risks putting the world organization up against a very tough situation. This is true because both Israel, which occupied the new part of the city, and Jordan, which occupied the old city, declare that they will oppose the implementation of the United Nations' decision by force if necessary. The United Nations has at present no military forces to use to carry out its decision; and it is a good guess that few, if any, of its members will come forward with offers to supply troops to carry out the plan."

The Foreign Minister of Israel, Mr. Sharett, attacked the plan as a direct blow at Israel, "cutting out the very heart of the country." Mr. James concluded his article with these ominous words: "It may turn out that the Assembly vote on Jerusalem was just about the worst blunder which has been committed by the United Nations. It is a dubious proposition for an international body to make decisions which it is not in a position to carry out. This is certainly true of this one. What will it lead to?" Since this decision, there has been much discussion in the United Nations on the subject; some compromise plans have been proposed and some attempts to alter the original decision have been made. In the meantime, the Israeli government has passed one resolution after another against the action of the United Nations.[10]

The "Perpetual Hatred" of the Arabs | 6

"They have said, Come, and let us cut them off from being a nation; that the name of Israel may be no more in remembrance."

Psalm 83:4

This is not the place to go into detail regarding the war in Sinai in 1967 which carried Israel forces to the Suez, nor to review the events that have just taken place resulting in the capture of practically all of the territory West of the Jordan by the Israeli forces.

Today there are approximately two million Jews within the narrow boundaries of the State of Israel: far more than were living in all of Palestine at the time of Christ.

On the evening of June 10, 1967, the Ambassador to the United Nations from Syria said something like this: "Why should we Arabs and Jews fight? Before Israel became a state, we dwelt together peaceably, and profitably. This is the way it ought to be, because, we are all of one race." This is truly so, because the Arabs and the Israelites are all descendants of Abraham, and recognize, of course, this historic fact. But while they are members of the same race, the Arabs have been hating Israel century after century. Indeed this began in the very days of the patriarchs when the foundations of Israel were being laid. In the sixteenth chapter of Genesis, in which is recorded the birth of Ishmael, we read that the angel of the Lord said to Hagar, the Egyptian handmaid, who was about to bear a son and to call his name Ishmael, "He will be a wild man; his hand will be against every man, and every man's hand against him; and he shall dwell in the presence of all his brethren" (Genesis 16:12). Leupold rightly translates the last clause, "He will dwell over against all his brethren," or, actually, "to the east of," which means "against the face of," and this "plainly involves hostility as in Job 1:11." Leupold further amplifies the point: "The unrestrained love of liberty on the part of these wild desert animals is further depicted in Job 39:5-8. Ishmael's descendants, the Arabs, roving over the wild expanses of the desert lands adjacent to Bible lands are still characterized by this trait. He cannot be said to be distinguished for amiability and love of peace. He personally shall be the aggressor against all others. Even in the matter of a dwelling place, this antagonistic spirit, brooking no restraint or interference shall express itself in his dwelling 'over against all his brethren'."¹ Notice the profound comment of St. Paul in Galatians 4:29. "But as then he that was born after the flesh persecuted him that was born after the Spirit, even so it is now."

We do not turn many pages in the book of Genesis before we come upon a record of another event which resulted in an additional hatred of the Jews, descendants of Jacob, and that in a double episode. First of all, Esau, despising his birthright, sold it to his twin brother, Jacob, for a bowl of porridge (Genesis 25:27-34). In the 27th chapter is the record of Jacob's deception of his father by which he received the greater paternal blessing, thereby cheating Esau, with the result that "Esau hated Jacob because of the blessing wherewith his father blessed him: and Esau said in his heart, The days of mourning for my father are at hand; then will I slay my brother Jacob." [(Genesis 27:41). Let me repeat here this dreadful concluding line, "I will slay my brother Jacob."] It should be remembered that Esau is often called Edom: "Now these are the generations of Esau, who is Edom" (Genesis 36:1) and the territory in which his descendants lived is frequently referred to as Mt. Seir. "And Jacob sent messengers before him to Esau his brother unto the land of Seir, the country of Edom" (Genesis 32:3). These words should be remembered as we shortly will be considering prophecies in which they will occur.

During the wanderings of Israel, before possession of the land, Moses sent messengers to the king of Edom, reminding him of his relationship to Israel, asking if they might pass through his country without hurting the crops or using the wells, a request that was emphatically refused (Numbers 20:14-21). The country of the Edomites extended from the Dead Sea to the Gulf of Aqaba. During the centuries that followed the descendants of Esau, these Edomites, as well as the Ishmaelites, were a perpetual nuisance, and sometimes a menace to the Israelites, no doubt in more ways than the historical books of the Old Testament have informed us. It is because of this antagonism of the Edomites that the book of Obadiah was written, in which Edom is reminded of "thy violence against thy brother Jacob" (verse 10).

The eighty-third Psalm speaks of the antagonism of Edom and her allies against Israel. Edom is mentioned first because of her prominence, no doubt, in these plots against Israel, and next to be named are the Ishmaelites. The Moabites dwelt directly East of the Dead Sea. Ammon was the territory occupied by the Ammonites and this is exactly the same word as the capital of Jordan today, Amman. The Philistines and the Tyrians lived on the coast. Assyria, of course, is today, in part, Iraq. Now we are ready for the Psalmist's plea. "Keep not thou silence, O God: hold not thy peace, and be not still, O God. For, lo, thine enemies make a tumult: and they that hate thee have lifted up the head. They have said, Come, and let us cut them off from being a nation; that the name of Israel may be no more in remembrance" (Psalm 83:1-4).

I do not want in any way to seem sensational, but this 4th verse is almost word for word what President Nasser has been saying for the last two or three years over his powerful radio station, that is, it is his determination to destroy Israel.[2]

This unceasing hatred on the part of the Arabs for Israel down through the centuries is most concisely admitted in such a standard work as the "World Almanac for 1965." "From the start Israel met with the opposition of the Arab League, which established headquarters in Damascus to enforce an economic boycott. Armed invasions were also begun in Syria, Egypt, Iraq, Lebanon, Saudi-Arabia and Jordan. Separate armistices with the Arab nations were signed in 1949, but no general peace settlement was obtained. The Arab nations continue policies of economic boycott, blockade in the Suez Canal, political warfare and local incitement."[3]

Before examining one final passage regarding these enemies of Israel, may I speak of an experience which I had in Jerusalem in 1937. I was entertained at tea one afternoon by the late Mr. Clark, then the head of the Barclay's Banks of the Near East, a devout student of the Scriptures and a man of great generosity to evangelical causes. During those days in Jerusalem, one would hear every day of some Jewish family living in a remote village that had been slain during the night by the Arabs, followed soon after discovery by the Jews burning some Arab village. As we talked in the garden that afternoon, shooting could be heard in the hills around Jerusalem. I remarked to Mr. Clark how tragic it was that these Arabs and Jews had to be engaged in such a continual feud, to which he at once replied, "Well, this is all set forth in the Scriptures." I should have told him, "Yes, I know," but instead of that I came much nearer to the truth by asking where this conflict is foretold in the Scriptures. He reached into his hip pocket and pulled out a Bible and began to read aloud to me the opening verses of the 35th chapter of Ezekiel. Let us have these words before us. "Moreover the word of Jehovah came unto me, saying, Son of man, set thy face against mount Seir, and prophesy against it, and say unto it, Thus saith the Lord Jehovah: Behold, I am against thee, O mount Seir, and I will stretch out my hand against thee, and I will make thee a desolation and an astonishment. I will lay thy cities waste, and thou shalt be desolate; and thou shalt know that I am Jehovah. Because thou hast had a perpetual enmity, and hast given over the children of Israel to the power of the sword in the time of their calamity, in the time of the iniquity of the end" (Ezekiel 35:1-5, A.R.V.).'

One should carefully note where this particular statement occurs. It is placed immediately before the great passage on the restoration of Israel to her land and her glorious conversion supplemented by the famous vision of the valley of dry bones, which, in turn, is followed by that graphic description of the invasion of Palestine of these godless powers and their overwhelming destruction. Consequently, this particular paragraph regarding Edom in Chapter 35 relates particularly to the events occurring at the end of this age, and what we have seen in the June of 1967 only adds evidence to the truthfulness of this ancient prophecy.

Cease Fire Lines — "War's Aftermath" Israel said war in the Middle East had wiped out past armistice pacts and indicated borders would have to change. Area overrun by Israeli forces is shown in light shading. Cease-fire in the Syrian area (cross) was accepted.

Jesus' Prediction About Jerusalem | **7**

"Jerusalem shall be trodden down of the Gentiles, until the times of the Gentiles be fufilled."

Luke 21:24

In St. Luke's account of the Olivet Discourse, there is a short but profound statement regarding the future of Jerusalem, which is taking on tremendous meaning. Indeed it now looks, unless there is some great reversal, as though it were fulfilled. The verse is as follows: "And they shall fall by the edge of the sword, and shall be led away captive into all the nations: and Jerusalem shall be trodden down of the Gentiles, until the times of the Gentiles be fulfilled" (Luke 21:24). There are three time-periods in this verse: the first is that of the destruction of Jerusalem under Titus, occurring forty years after our Lord uttered these words—"they shall be led away captive into all nations." The second period extends from then, and perhaps long before that, to the end of this age, to the end of "the times of the Gentiles." Finally, there is that hour or day or year, in which there comes to an end the times of the Gentiles, which must be a part of the last days of this age.

To this verse the church fathers gave no consideration, as to most of the great Olivet Discourse. The Reformation commentators, which would include Calvin also, rarely interested in eschatology, ignored it. We might profitably here review what some of the more recent commentators have said on this passage. Godet, after an excellent defense of the authenticity of these lines, makes the time of the Gentiles simply "the whole period during which God shall approach with His grace the Gentiles who have been hitherto strangers to His kingdom." But this does not in any way even hint what the verse so plainly teaches, that there will come a time when Jerusalem will be no longer "trodden down of the Gentiles." J. J .Van Oosterzee in the Lange series of commentaries has one helpful line in which he says that in this statement there is "a thought of the restoration of Jerusalem (which gleams through)." Bishop W. B. Jones, in the "Speaker's Commentary on the New Testament," after giving the views of a number of commentators, says that the idea that this refers to "the period during which the Gentiles are permitted to occupy Jerusalem and to be ministers of God's judgment upon the Jews," accords best with the Greek. As many others do, he introduces the famous statement of Romans 11:25, that "blindness in part is happened to Israel, until the fullness of the Gentiles be come in." H. D. M. Spence in the "Pulpit Commentary" recognized that "these few words carry on the prophecy close to the days of the end, when the Lord will return," and adds the interesting comment that "these words separate the prophecy of Jesus which belongs solely to the ruin of the city and temple ... and begins a short prophetic description of the coming of the Son of Man in glory."

Coming into the twentieth century, Alfred Plummer in his superb commentary in the "International Critical Commentary" series gives six different interpretations of "the times of the Gentiles." He adopts the first and the sixth himself, namely, that it refers to "seasons for executing the divine judgments," and times of "possessing the privileges which the Jews had forfeited." He mentions a number of Gentile nations which, in centuries past, have trampled upon the city, but he does not hint what will take place when this period is concluded. Lonsdale Ragg accepts this idea, but adds what the earlier commentators, of course, knew nothing about. He seems to think that the verse has been fulfilled, namely, that this trampling down by Romans, Turks, Crusaders, etc., continued "until in 1916 the 'Last Crusade' treated her with a reverence and a gentleness unknown in more than thirty centuries of warfare." Nevertheless, Jerusalem was still under the power of Gentile nations. J. M. Creed says that "the meaning seems to be that the Gentiles have a fixed period during which they will be allowed to lord it over Jerusalem." Then he says that one should compare Ezekiel 33, and that the statement in one way may be considered as equivalent to Mark 13:10.

The famous Lutheran New Testament scholar, Dr. R. C. H. Lenski, in his truly superb commentary on Luke's Gospel, written in 1934, introduces some modern data in saying, "The Zionist movement today is the latest attempt of the Jews to repossess their land, and it has failed." (It is dangerous to go outside of the Word of God, instead of attempting to simply state what the Scriptures say.) He then gives a translation which I have not found anywhere else, stating that the Greek verb is *durative* and the phrase should be translated "Jerusalem shall continue to be trampled by the Gentiles" and then insists that this situation will continue to the time of the Second Advent. He follows Luther in saying, "God is done with the Jews as a nation." Dr. Norval Geldenhuys in his recent work on Luke's Gospel (1951) introduces something which no one would think the text even implied when he says that "Christ nowhere implies that the times of the Gentiles will be followed by Jewish dominion over the nations," and rejects the idea of a Jewish kingdom.

The one commentator, as far as my knowledge of this literature extends, who most satisfactorily deals with this final clause, is Bishop J. C. Ryle, in his great work, "Expository Thoughts on the Gospels."

"A fixed period is here foretold, during which Jerusalem was to be given over into the hands of Gentile rulers, and the Jews were to have no dominion over their ancient city. A fixed period is likewise foretold which was to be the time of the Gentiles' visitation, the time during which they were to enjoy privileges, and occupy a position something like that of Israel in ancient days ... Both periods are one day to end. Jerusalem is to be once more restored to its ancient inhabitants. The Gentiles, because of their hardness and unbelief, are to be stripped of their privileges and endure just judgments of God But the times of the Gentiles are not yet run out. We ourselves are living within them at the present day.

"The subject before us is a very affecting one, and ought to raise within us great searchings of heart. While the nations of Europe are absorbed in political conflicts and worldly business, the sands of their hourglass are ebbing away. While governments are disputing about secular things, and parliaments can hardly condescend to find a place for religion in their discussions, their days are numbered in the mind of God. Yet a few years, and 'the times of the Gentiles will be fulfilled.' Their days of visitation will be past and gone. Their misused privileges will be taken away. The judgments of God shall fall on them. They shall be cast aside as vessels in which God has no pleasure. Their dominion shall crumble away, and their vaunted institutions shall fall to pieces. The Jews shall be restored. The Lord Jesus shall come again in power and great glory. The kingdom of this world shall become the kingdom of our God and of His Christ, and 'the times of the Gentiles' shall come to an end.

"Happy is he who knows these things, and lives the life of faith in the Son of God! He is the man, and he only, who is ready for the great things coming on this earth, and the appearing of the Lord Jesus Christ. The kingdom to which he belongs, is the only kingdom which shall never be destroyed. The King whom he serves, is the only King whose dominion shall never be taken away" (Daniel 2:44; 7:14).[1] (This is not to be found in a recently published "Anniversary Edition" of Ryle's work.)

I would like to introduce here some words of my own which were written in 1952, after quoting this passage from Bishop Ryle. "I am not an alarmist, and I trust through the years I have never attached to any world event a prophetic significance that was not justified; but it seems to me that almost any day or night this prophecy of our Lord could be fulfilled. Already there are more Jews living in Jerusalem than there were Jews living in the whole of Palestine at the dawn of this century. Furthermore, there is a government of a newborn nation in the modern city of Jerusalem—Israel. One hundred feet of no man's land, some barbed wire fences, and a few machine guns manned by a mere handful of Arabs —these are all that keep the Jews from fully occupying this city and setting up their government there.

"Why the Jews do not go in and take that city, I do not know; they certainly could do it. It may be that God will not permit this for some time. It may be that the Jews would enter into the city, capture it, attempt to set up their government, and bring down upon themselves the power and wrath of the nations of the earth, and then this prophecy would not yet be fulfilled; for when it is fulfilled, Jerusalem will never again be trodden down of the Gentiles. I am only saying that, for the first time in all these two thousand years, we are amazingly near to the possibility of the fulfillment of this verse."[2]

Since the above was first composed, two altogether different decisions have been made, officially, by the Ministry of Foreign Affairs for Israel, Mr. Abba Eban. In the week in which the Old City (of Jerusalem) was seized it was affirmed that this part of their newly conquered territory they would never return to the Arabs. On Tuesday, June the 20th, 1967, Mr. Eban stated that Israel would be willing to see Jerusalem internationalized. If this should happen the city would then be still under Gentile control, and the fulfillment of Luke 21:24 would be indefinitely postponed.

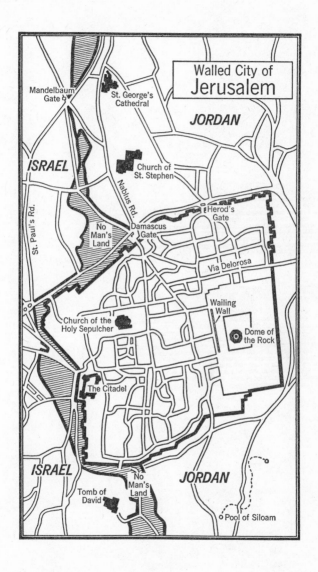

Walled City of
Jerusalem

Mandelbaum
Gate

St. George's
Cathedral

JORDAN

ISRAEL

Church of
St. Stephen

St. Paul's Rd.

Nablus Rd.

No
Man's
Land

Damascus
Gate

Herod's
Gate

Via Delorosa

Wailing
Wall

Church of the
Holy Sepulcher

Dome of
the Rock

The Citadel

ISRAEL

No
Man's
Land

JORDAN

Tomb of
David

Pool of Siloam

Jerusalem ... What Next? | **8**

"For the Lord hath chosen Zion:
he hath desired it for his habitation."

Psalm 132:13

Jerusalem has not only been in its previous history the unrivalled center of God's redemptive work but is also to be the center of the universal activities of the nations of the earth at the end of this age. It is the place to which Christ himself will descend at his Second Advent. Priesthood in the Bible begins in Jerusalem with the appearance of Melchizedek. The only intended capital for the kingdom of Israel was Jerusalem, the city of David. This is the city in which most of the prophets ministered or concerning which they spoke. Here our Lord was crucified and rose from the dead. Here the Holy Spirit descended on the day of Pentecost, and here will great events take place at the end of this age—events of international significance.

A City That Will Know Perpetual War

At the end of the great prophecy of the seventy weeks, Daniel in referring to this very city, says that "unto the end shall be war; desolations are determined" (Daniel 9:26,A.R.V.). Professor Leupold, one of the great Biblical scholars of this generation, has an excellent remark concerning this particular phrase. "War, which is getting more and more to be the mark of the times, and which is growing increasingly more cruel, shall go on to 'the very end'. The oppositional statement, 'destined desolations,' points to the inevitable accompaniment of all wars, which in this last instance, it would appear, will be all the more in evidence. For we have witnessed the fact that, as time went on, the havoc wrought by war is more thoroughgoing than ever. Men are, therefore, not to be surprised at finding wars and desolations toward the end. In fact, they are one form of evil that dominates the last great 'tribulation', to speak the language of the New Testament in this connection."[1]

Jerusalem, a Burdensome Stone

There is a truly profound statement regarding Jerusalem as an enigma for the nations at the end of this age, which I am afraid is too seldom considered. It is at the beginning of the 12th chapter of Zechariah. "Behold, I will make Jerusalem a cup of reeling unto all the peoples round about, and upon Judah also shall it be in the siege against Jerusalem. And it shall come to pass in that day, that I will make Jerusalem a burdensome stone for all the peoples; all that burden themselves with it shall be sore wounded; and all the nations of the earth shall be gathered together against it" (Zechariah 12:2,3,A.R.V.).

Dr. Charles H. Wright of Trinity College, Dublin, not a believer in the literal interpretation of prophecy has, nevertheless, in his great series of Bampton Lectures on Zechariah, well stated that this idea of a burdensome stone clearly implies that "in vain should all the nations round about seek to fit the stone of Jerusalem into any of the political structures which they might seek to erect. All their efforts to raise that burdensome stone would prove injurious to themselves."[2]

A TEMPLE TO BE BUILT IN JERUSALEM

Toward the conclusion of Daniel's famous prophecy of the seventy weeks, we read that the great enemy of God will "cause the sacrifice and the oblation to cease" (Daniel 9:27), and at the very end of the same prophetic book we read of a time when "the continual burnt-offering shall be taken away, and the abomination that maketh desolate set up" (12:11,A.R.V.). It is to this event that our Lord directs the attention of His disciples, and the entire Christian Church, when in the midst of the Olivet Discourse He says: "When therefore ye see the abomination of desolation, which was spoken of through Daniel the prophet, standing in the holy place (let him that readeth understand)" (Matthew 24:15, A.R.V.). See also Mark 13:14. Incidentally, I believe this is the only time, in referring to any Old Testament passages, our Lord said, "Let him that readeth understand."

It is to this event that the Apostle Paul also must be referring in his classic unfolding of the truth concerning the Man of Sin, of whom he writes "... except the falling away come first, and the man of sin be revealed, the son of perdition, he that opposeth and exalteth himself against all that is called God or that is worshipped; so that he sitteth in the temple of God, setting himself forth as God" (II Thessalonians 2:3,4, A.R.V.). This certainly implies a rebuilding of the Temple in Jerusalem, which was destroyed by Titus in A.D. 70. Here today stands the Dome of the Rock, a Moslem mosque.

Presumably this Temple will be built by the Jews, because the texts we have just quoted all imply that this enemy of God will desecrate the sanctuary. The whole phenomenon is looked upon as something terrible to be dreaded, a catastrophe to the Jews. The Temple certainly is not to be built by Antichrist; for he would never introduce a sacrifice which he himself would cause to cease. In bringing to an end the sacrifice ritual of the Jews, now back in Palestine, he will set himself up as God.[3]

The Two Witnesses to Appear in the City of Jerusalem

In the 11th chapter of the Book of Revelation, there is a definite statement that for three and one-half years, the first half of the period of tribulation, two witnesses will appear bearing testimony probably to the Gospel, who when their testimony is finished will be slain by Antichrist. Then we come upon a most astonishing statement. Their dead bodies are left lying in the street of this great city, which is so apostate and wicked that, as in the days of Isaiah, it is spiritually called Sodom and Egypt. "From among the peoples and tribes and tongues and nations do men look upon their dead bodies three days and a half, and suffer not their dead bodies to be laid in a tomb. And they that dwell on the earth rejoice over them, and make merry; and they shall send gifts one to another; because these two prophets tormented them that dwell on the earth" (Revelation 11:8,10,A.R.V.).

The outstanding New Testament scholar, Robert Govett, wrote of this passage more than one hundred years ago (1864): "The word translated 'look upon,' 'blepo,' denotes not merely the nations seeing them, but their directing their eyes to this great sight and gazing upon them . . . 'But how,' it is asked, 'is it conceivable that men all over the earth should be rejoicing at the news when only three days and a half intervene between their death and resurrection?' . . . Is it not perfectly conceivable if the electric telegraph shall then have extended itself at the rate it has done of late years?"[4]

We today know how this passage will be literally fulfilled—by television. Lenski has, in my opinion, one of the most profound comments on this passage in all the vast literature of this part of the Apocalypse when he says, "The wicked world cannot let them alone and simply pass on in its obduracy. Even when it is finally and utterly silenced, the obdurate world cannot dismiss the divine testimony. It must talk about it, bring everybody to look at the voiceless lips. Though dead, these lips still speak (Hebrews 11:14). Those who spurn the Word, never get rid of it. Their very rejoicing over its silencing keeps them busy with the Word."[5]

NEW BOUNDARIES FOR THE CITY

There is no doubt about it that at the end of the 31st chapter of Jeremiah, we have some boundaries for the city of Jerusalem that have never been true for any particular period of its history. "Behold, the days come, saith Jehovah, that the city shall be built to Jehovah from the tower of Hananel unto the gate of the corner.

112

And the measuring line shall go out further straight onward unto the hill Gareb, and shall turn about unto Goah" (Jeremiah 31:38-40, A.R.V.). I do not want to elaborate upon this but two short statements from nineteenth century students of prophecy are worth repeating. "By this extension the places which were unholy will have nothing unholy to cast out." "There could be no greater victory of the kingdom of God over the world than if this strictest antithesis to the holy city, this image of hill, was included within the holy city."[6]

A Final Siege of Jerusalem

With all of the wonderful promises concerning this city in the Old Testament writings, we must not deliberately ignore the terrible words appearing near the close of the book of Zechariah regarding a final and temporarily successful siege of this city. "Behold, a day of Jehovah cometh, when thy spoil shall be divided in the midst of thee. For I will gather all nations against Jerusalem to battle; and the city shall be taken, and the houses rifled, and the women ravished; and half of the city shall go forth into captivity, and the residue of the people shall not be cut off from the city. Then shall Jehovah go forth, and fight against those nations, as when he fought in the day of battle" (Zechariah 14:1-3,A.R.V.).

No one has commented upon this important

passage with greater insight than the late Dr. David Baron, in his superbly rich exposition of the "Prophecies of Zechariah." Writing as far back as 1918, Baron rightly says, "There will be at first, as compared with the whole nation, only a representative minority in Palestine, and a Jewish state will be probably formed, either under the suzerainty of one of the Great Powers, or under international protection . . . A large number more from all parts of the world will in all probability soon be gathered; but we shall only be able to speak of a restoration of the Jews as an accomplished fact when Palestine becomes by international consent (to quote from the Zionist programme) the 'openly recognized and legally assured home' of the Jews, i.e., when the Jews are once more acknowledged as a nation with a land of their own to which they might go.

". . . After a brief interval of prosperity there comes a night of anguish. What occasions the darkest hour in the night of Israel's sad history since their rejection of Christ is the gathering of the nations and the siege predicted in this Chapter."

To continue Baron's description of the terrible battle that we know will be fought: "Infuriated, probably by the faithfulness to the covenant God of their fathers on the part of the godly remnant who shall then be found in the land, the Anti-Christ forms the purpose of utterly and finally exterminating this people, who can never cease, even in apostasy and unbelief, to be witnesses

114

for the living God and His truth. The armies of the confederated nations, the very flower of their strength, are marshalled together in Palestine, their watchword being, 'Come let us cut them off from being a nation, that the name of Israel may be no more in remembrance.'

". . . They march in triumph through the land, easily treading down all opposition. And now the enemy in overwhelming force and irresistible fury attacks Jerusalem, which is soon at his mercy. The city is taken, and the 'spoil' or booty leisurely 'divided in the midst' of her, without fear on the part of the enemy of interruption or molestation. There ensue scenes of cruel brutality, and lust, and horrors, which usually accompany the sack of cities by enraged enemies, only intensified in this particular case by the accumulated hatred of these confederated hosts against this land and people. Half of the remaining population in the city is dragged forth into captivity, and there is but a small and wretched fear on the part of the enemy of interruption or the enemy are also devoted to destruction." "Proclaim ye this among the nations: prepare war; stir up the mighty men; let all the men of war draw near, let them come up. Let the nations bestir themselves, and come up to the valley of Jehoshaphat; for there will I sit to judge all the nations round about" (Joel 3:9,12,A.R.V.). "And it shall be as when a hungry man dreameth, and, behold, he eateth; but he awaketh, and his soul is empty: or as when a thirsty man dreameth, and behold, he drinketh; but he awaketh, and, behold, he is faint, and his soul hath appetite: so shall the multitude of all the nations be, that fight against mount Zion" (Isaiah 29:8,A.R.V.).[7]

PEACE IN RELATION TO JERUSALEM

Jerusalem in its very name, the city of peace, is continually connected in the Old Testament prophets with this matter of peace within its own walls and peace through the one who will reign there. While Isaiah mentions this matter of peace in relation to Jerusalem in a number of prophecies, he develops the theme most fully at the end of his profound unveilings of the future. "Rejoice ye with Jerusalem, and be glad for her, all ye that love her: rejoice for joy with her, all ye that mourn over her; that ye may suck and be satisfied with the breasts of her consolations; that ye may milk out, and be delighted with the abundance of her glory. For thus saith Jehovah, Behold, I will extend peace to her like a river, and the glory of the nations like an overflowing stream: and ye shall suck thereof; ye shall be borne upon the side, and shall be dandled upon the knees" (Isaiah 66:10-12,A.R.V.). "And the work of the righteousness shall be peace; and the effect of righteousness, quietness and confidence for ever. And my people shall abide in a peaceable habitation, and in safe dwellings, and in quiet, resting-places" (Isaiah 32:17,18,A.R.V.). "Look upon Zion, the city of our solemnities:

thine eyes shall see Jerusalem a quiet habitation, a tent that shall not be removed, the stakes whereof shall never be plucked up, neither shall any of the cords thereof be broken" (Isaiah 33:20,A.R.V.).

Haggai has a most significant statement regarding this matter of peace when he says that "in this place will I give peace, saith the Lord of hosts" (Haggai 2:9). It is echoed by Zechariah when he says that when the king comes to Zion "he shall speak peace unto the heathen (nations): and his dominion shall be from sea even to sea, and from the river even to the ends of the earth" (Zechariah 9:10).

Front line troops at the Western Wall (Wailing Wall). Center is the Israeli army chaplain holding the sacred scroll and shofar (ram's horn).

Jerusalem's Final Glory | 9

"Rejoice ye with Jerusalem, and be glad with her, all ye that love her: rejoice for joy with her, all ye that mourn for her: ... For thus said the Lord, Behold, I will extend peace to her like a river."

Isaiah 66:10,12

Many cities and geographical areas are referred to in the prophetic Scriptures but of none of them are there any predictions of future glory, except in relation to the city of Jerusalem. Concerning this city the prophets seem almost unable to find words adequate for expressing the ultimate wondrous state of Jerusalem.

Isaiah at the very beginning of his prophecies refers to Jerusalem as a city that "afterward ... shalt be called the city of righteousness, a faithful town" (Isaiah 1:26,A.R.V.). Then he goes on to say, "Zion shall be redeemed with justice, and her converts with righteousness" (Isaiah 1:27,A.R.V.). Let us not forget that the Hebrew word translated "righteousness" is "zedek," which forms part of the word of "Melchizedek," for which reason the writer of the Epistle to the Hebrews calls this mysterious person "King of righteousness" in Hebrews 7:2. Then Isaiah continues: "And it shall come to pass in the latter days, that the mountain of Jehovah's house shall be established on the top of the mountains, and shall be exalted above all the hills; and all nations shall flow unto it. And many people shall go and say, Come ye, and let us go up to the mountain of Jehovah, to the house of the God of Jacob; and he will teach us of his ways, and we will walk in his paths: for out of Zion shall go forth the law, and the word of Jehovah from Jerusalem" (Isaiah 2:2,3,A.R.V.). The movement here is first centripetal, and then centrifugal. Of this time the same prophet later speaks in that famous prophecy, "Nations shall come to thy light, and kings to the brightness of thy rising" (Isaiah 60:3,A.R.V.). And, in the same chapter, after other remarkable utterances, we read, "The sons of them that afflicted thee shall come bending unto thee; ... and they shall call thee The city of Jehovah, The Zion of the Holy One of Israel" (verse 14,A.R.V.). "The nations shall see thy righteousness, and all kings thy glory; and ... thou shalt also be a crown of beauty in the hand of Jehovah, and a royal diadem in the hand of thy God" (Isaiah 62:2,3,A.R.V.). "Behold, Jehovah hath proclaimed unto the end of the earth, Say ye to the daughter of Zion, Behold, thy salvation cometh; behold, his reward is with him. And they shall call them The holy people, The redeemed of Jehovah: and thou shall be called Sought out, A city not forsaken" (Isaiah 62:11,12,A.R.V.); "For I know their works and their thoughts: the time cometh, that I will gather all nations and tongues; and they shall come, and shall see my glory. And I will set a sign among them, and I will send such an escape of them unto the nations, to Tarshish, Pul, and Lud, that draw the bow, to Tubal and Javan, to the isles afar off, that have not heard my fame, neither have seen my glory; and they shall declare my glory among the nations. And they shall bring all your brethren out of all the nations for an oblation unto Jehovah, upon horses, and in chariots, and in litters, and upon mules, and upon dromedaries, to my holy mountain Jerusalem, saith Jehovah, as the children of Israel bring their oblation in a clean vessel into the house of Jehovah. And of them also will I take for priests and for Levites, saith Jehovah" (Isaiah 66:18-21,A.R.V.). "Thus saith Jehovah, The labor of Egypt, and the merchandise of Ethiopia, and the Sabeans, men of stature, shall come over unto thee, and they shall be thine: they shall go after thee; in chains they shall come over; and they shall fall down unto thee, they shall make supplication unto thee, saying, Surely God is in thee; and there is none else, there is no God. Look unto me, and be ye saved, all the ends of the earth; for I am God, and there is none else. By myself have I sworn, the word is gone forth from my mouth in righteousness, and shall not return, that unto me every knee shall bow, every tongue shall swear. Only in Jehovah, it is said of me, is righteousness and strength; even to him shall men come; and all they that were incensed against him shall be put to shame" (Isaiah 45:14,22-25,A.R.V.); "Lo, these shall come from far; and, lo, these from the north and from the west; and these from the land of Sinim" (Isaiah 49:12,A.R.V.); "Jehovah is exalted; for he dwelleth on high: he hath filled Zion with justice and righteousness" (Isaiah 33:5); "For thus saith Jehovah: We have heard a voice of trembling, of fear, and not of peace" (Jeremiah 30:5,A.R.V.); "Thus saith Jehovah: I am returned unto Zion, and will dwell in the midst of Jerusalem: and Jerusalem shall be called The city of truth; and the mountain of Jehovah of hosts, The holy mountain. Thus saith Jehovah of hosts: There shall yet old men and old women dwell in the streets of Jerusalem, every man with his staff in his hand for very age. And the streets of the city shall be full of boys and girls playing in the streets thereof. Thus saith Jehovah of hosts: If it be marvelous in the eyes of the remnant of this people in those days, should it also be marvelous in mine eyes? saith Jehovah of hosts. Yea, many peoples and strong nations shall come to seek Jehovah of hosts in Jerusalem, and to entreat the favor of Jehovah" (Zechariah 8:3-6,22,A.R.V.). There are many other passages predicting Israel's turning to God which I am not listing here.

In the great work by Nathaniel West, "The Thousand Years in Both Testaments," there is a tremendous statement by the great German theologian of the nineteenth century, Riehm, regarding Israel's return and conversion. "The entrance of the nations into the Kingdom of God," said Riehm, "follows Israel's conversion. They are prepared for it by judicial displays of Jehovah's majesty in the destruction of the enemies of His Kingdom. Those who are spared are filled with fear and trembling at His presence. It is the deliverance of Israel effected by these judgments, and the Messianic salvation thus brought to her people, which first awake in the nations the desire to belong to God whom they have thus learned to know as the only Helper. There is a full recognition of the equality of the Gentiles with the Jews in their relation to Christ and the blessings of salvation, yet this does not exclude the idea that, without prejudice to this equality, Israel as a nation may take a high position in the perfected Kingdom of Christ. The entry of the nations in the Kingdom of God in their natural fellowship with Israel are realized through Israel as the special possessor of these blessings."[1]

When Jerusalem is cleansed of all of its shame and pollutions, it will then become what it was originally intended to be, a holy city. "And it shall come to pass, that he that is left in Zion, and he that remaineth in Jerusalem, shall be called holy, even every one that is written among the living in Jerusalem; when the Lord shall have washed away the filth of the daughters of Zion, and shall have purged the blood of Jerusalem from the midst thereof, by the spirit of justice, and by the spirit of burning" (Isaiah 4:3,4,A.R.V.).

Israel's greatest characteristics in those days will all pertain to her genuine spirituality. "Therefore say, Thus saith the Lord Jehovah: I will gather you from the peoples, and assemble you out of the countries where ye have been scattered, and I will give you the land of Israel. And they shall come thither, and they shall take away all the detestable things thereof and all the abominations thereof from thence. And I will give them one heart, and I will put a new spirit within you; and I will take the stony heart out of their flesh, and will give them a heart of flesh; that they may walk in my statutes, and keep mine ordinances, and do them: and they shall be my people, and I will be their God" (Ezekiel 11:17-20,A.R.V.). "Behold, I will gather them out of all the countries, whither I have driven them in mine anger, and in my wrath, and in great indignation; and I will bring them again unto this place, and I will cause them to dwell safely. And they shall be my people, and I will be their God: and I will give them one heart and one way, that they may fear me for ever, for the good of them, and of their children after them: and I will make an everlasting covenant with them, that I will not turn away from following them, to do them good, and I will put my fear in their hearts, that they may not depart from me. Yea, I will rejoice over them to do them good, and I will plant them in this land assuredly with my whole heart and with my whole soul" (Jeremiah 32:37-41,A.R.V.). Such a restoration of spirituality is connected by the prophet Isaiah with that great prediction concerning the Spirit of the Lord resting upon the Messiah, "to appoint unto them that mourn in Zion, to give unto them a garland for ashes, the oil of joy for mourning, the garment of praise for the spirit of heaviness; that they may be called trees of righteousness, the planting of Jehovah, that he may be glorified" (Isaiah 61:3,A.R.V.). "And the nations shall see thy righteousness, and all kings thy glory; and thou shalt be called by a new name, which the mouth of Jehovah shall name. Thou shalt also be a crown of beauty in the hand of Jehovah, and a royal diadem in the hand of thy God ... Behold, Jehovah hath proclaimed unto the end of the earth, Say ye to the daughter of Zion, Behold, thy salvation cometh; behold, his reward is with him, and his recompense before him. And they shall call them The holy people, The redeemed of Jehovah: and thou shalt be called Sought out, A city not forsaken" (Isaiah 62:2,3,11,12,A.R.V.). "And many nations shall go and say, Come ye, and let us go up to the mountain of Jehovah, and to the house of the God of Jacob; and he will teach us of his ways, and we will walk in his paths. For out of Zion shall go forth the law, and the word of Jehovah from Jerusalem; and he will judge between many peoples, and will decide concerning strong nations afar off: and they shall beat their swords into plowshares, and their spears into pruning-hooks; nation shall not lift up sword against nation, neither shall they learn war any more" (Micah 4:2,3,A.R.V.), "Thus saith Jehovah: I am returned unto Zion, and will dwell in the midst of Jerusalem: and Jerusalem shall be called The city of truth; and the mountain of Jehovah of hosts, The holy mountain. Thus saith Jehovah of hosts: there shall yet old men and old women dwell in the streets of Jerusalem, every man with his staff in his hand for very age. And the streets of the city shall be full of boys and girls playing in the streets thereof. Thus saith Jehovah of hosts: If it be marvelous in the eyes of the remnant of this people in those days, should it also be marvellous in mine eyes? saith Jehovah of hosts. Thus saith Jehovah of hosts: It shall yet come to pass, that there shall come peoples, and the inhabitants of many cities; and the inhabitants of one city shall go to another, saying, Let us go speedily to entreat the favor of Jehovah, and to seek Jehovah of hosts: I will go also. Yea, many peoples and strong nations shall come to seek Jehovah of hosts in Jerusalem, and to entreat the favor of Jehovah. Thus saith Jehovah of hosts: In those days it shall come to pass, that ten men shall take hold, out of all the languages of the nations, they shall take hold of the skirt of him that is a Jew, saying, We will go with you, for we have heard that God is with you" (Zechariah 8:3-6,20-23,A.R.V.).

There is one factor related to Israel's ultimate glory that is too rarely commented upon, and that is, the presence of David's greater son in her midst. This is expressed briefly by Jeremiah, "they shall serve the Lord their God, and David their king, whom I will raise up unto them" (Jeremiah 30:9), but is more elaborately dwelt upon by Ezekiel, as for instance, "And I will set up one shepherd over them, and he shall feed them, even my servant David; he shall feed them, and he shall be their shepherd" (Ezekiel 34:23). This statement is more fully developed in the chapter immediately preceding the prophecies regarding the invasion of Gog and Magog. "And say unto them, Thus saith the Lord Jehovah: Behold, I will take the children of Israel from among the nations, whither they are gone, and will gather them on every side, and bring them into their own land: and I will make them one nation in the land, upon the mountains of Israel; and one king shall be king to them all; and they shall be no more two nations, neither shall they be divided into two kingdoms any more at all; neither shall they defile themselves any more with their idols, nor with their detestable things, nor with any of their transgressions; but I will save them out of all their dwelling-places, wherein they have sinned, and will cleanse them: so shall they be my people, and I will be their God. And my servant David shall be king over them; and they all shall have one shepherd: they shall also walk in mine ordinances, and observe my statutes, and do them" (Ezekiel 37:21-24,A.R.V.). Keil, with his usual conciseness, has said regarding this Davidic prophecy, "The true return of the Lord cannot take place without a return to David their king since God has promised the kingdom to David and his seed forever. This king David, however, is none other than the Messiah . . . The return was not to take place until the end of the days which does not denote the future generally but always the closing future of the kingdom of God, commencing with the coming of the Messiah.'"

JERUSALEM IN RELATION TO PEACE

It is natural, almost inevitable, that this city whose very name expresses the idea of peace, should be definitely related to the subject of peace in the prophecies concerning her ultimate glory. This is of a two-fold nature. There is first of all the prophecies promising peace for Jerusalem, and how little of that she has seen! Thus Isaiah, in a more or less general way, says "And the work of righteousness shall be peace; and the effect of righteousness, quietness and confidence for ever. And my people shall abide in a peaceable habitation, and in safe dwellings, and in quiet resting-places" (Isaiah 32:17,18,A.R.V.). More specifically, he relates this coming and permanent peace of Jerusalem in Isaiah 33:20.

This theme of peace for Jerusalem is brought to a great climax by the prophet at the very end of his remarkable series of profound predictions in Isaiah 66:10-12. Ezekiel also makes the point clearly: "And I, Jehovah, will be their God, and my servant David prince among them; I, Jehovah, have spoken it. And I will make with them a covenant of peace, and will cause evil beasts to cease out of the land and they shall dwell securely in the wilderness, and sleep in the woods. And I will make them and the places round about my hill a blessing; and I will cause the shower to come down in its season; there shall be showers of blessing" (Ezekiel 34:24-26,A.R.V.). "Moreover I will make a covenant of peace with them; it shall be an everlasting covenant with them; and I will place them, and multiply them, and will set my sanctuary in the midst of them for evermore" (Ezekiel 37:26,A.R.V.).

Not only is peace promised as the prevailing condition in Jerusalem in the days to come, but it is through the city of Jerusalem, it seems, that peace will come to the nations of the earth. "And I will cut off the chariot from Ephraim, and the horse from Jerusalem; and the battle bow shall be cut off; and he shall speak peace unto the nations: and his dominion shall be from sea to sea, and from the River to the ends of the earth" (Zechariah 9:10,A.R.V.). "The latter glory of this house shall be greater than the former, saith Jehovah of hosts; and in this place will I give peace, saith Jehovah of hosts" (Haggai 2:9,A.R.V.).

The City of Peace will bestow peace upon the whole earth when the Prince of Peace there reigns with the government upon his shoulders. Righteousness will be sovereign when the King of Righteousness has judged the world in righteousness. In that city as it first appears in history was seen a priest of the Most High God: in the age to come it will as a city have priestly functions in leading men to God. The Holy City will be the center of a holy humanity. To no city on earth have such titles of glory and honor been divinely given; to no city has been such guilt attached as to it—this city which crucified our Lord. Of no city are such prophecies of tragedy and tribulation uttered; toward this city will the armies of the earth march in hatred of God's peace. Toward that same city will nations move, seeking the law of the Lord; from that city will flow blessings to the whole earth. Satan hates this city. Christ wept over it. The Holy Spirit descended upon its believers. The nations will be irresistibly drawn to it for war. Christ will there reign. And Heaven will bring to a glorious and eternal fulfillment all the promises relating to it.

On the tremendous events of today (and tomorrow) occurring in the Mid-East, it is only the Bible that gives us any prophetic foreannouncements. There is absolutely nothing about these great events in Plato or Aristotle—in fact, Athens and all that ancient Greece stood for do not even come into the picture. Though Palestine was included in one of the provinces of the Roman empire, neither Cicero, nor Virgil, nor any other Roman writer of that day, has any passage that can be called prophetic in regard to the events of the Mid East. Even the geographer, Strabo, though he has scores of references to Jerusalem and other geographical loci in that area does not anywhere become a prophet of Palestine's future. Actually, even the Jewish writer, Josephus, of that first century, when the destiny of Jerusalem for centuries to come was being determined, makes no statement, I believe, regarding the return of the Jews to the land of their fathers. Nor will we find this in the pages of the great writers of the centuries to follow, not in Dante, or Shakespeare, or Goethe. It is only this divine word that in a day like this is the unquenchable lamp unto our feet and light unto our pathway.

We can hardly close this chapter more appropriately than simply to quote that great Psalm regarding this very matter of the peace of Jerusalem.

"I was glad when they said unto me,
Let us go unto the house of Jehovah.
Our feet are standing
Within thy gates, O Jerusalem,
Jerusalem, that are builded
As a city that is compact together;
Whither the tribes go up,
    even the tribes of Jehovah,
For an ordinance for Israel,
To give thanks unto the name of Jehovah.

For there are set thrones for judgment,
The thrones of the house of David.
Pray for peace of Jerusalem:
They shall prosper that love thee.
Peace be within thy walls,
And prosperity within thy palaces.
For my brethren and companions' sakes,
I will now say, Peace be within thee.
For the sake of the house of Jehovah our God
I will seek thy good" (Psalm 122,A.R.V.).

Israeli **Prime** Minister Levi Eshkol standing at the Western Wall (Wailing Wall) in the Old City of Jerusalem. By him is the Chief of the Central Command, Brig. Gen. Uzi Narkiss.

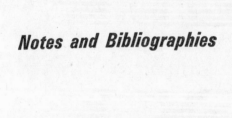

Notes and Bibliographies

Chapter 2

1. H.C. Leupold: "Exposition of Genesis," Columbus, 1942, pp. 441,519. With the kind permission of the publishers, the Wartburg Press, Columbus, Ohio.

2. The additional principal passages in which Palestine is spoken of as a gift of God to Israel are: Genesis 28:4; 35:12; Deuteronomy 2:12; 3:18; 12:1; 28:52; Joshua 21:43; 24:13; Numbers 32:7,9; I Kings 8:34,40,48; 14:15; II Kings 21:8; II Chronicles 6:25,31,38; Jeremiah 3:18; 16:15; 30:3; Ezekiel 36:28.

3. On the names of Palestine, see, e.g., J. Bannister: "A Survey of the Holy Land," London, 1844, pp. 9-12. I would here call attention to an article of mine, "Israel in her Promised Land," in "Christianity Today," December 24, 1956, Vol. I. The opposite position was discussed by Dr. Oswald T. Allis, in the same issue. For a recent discussion of these promises, see John F. Walvoord: "Israel in Prophecy," Grand Rapids, 1962, pp. 63-79.

Chapter 3

1. It is to be regretted that such a truly great interpreter of the Old Testament as Dr. C. F. Keil should interpret this passage with the confusing thesis that no real return to Palestine is here prophesied. "The land which will flow like streams of divine blessings is not Palestine, but the domain of the Christian Church, or the

earth, so far as it has received the blessings of Christianity. The people which cultivates this land is the Christian Church, so far as it stands in living faith, and produces fruits of the Holy Ghost." C. F. Keil: "The Twelve Minor Prophets," Eng. translation, Vol. I, Edinburgh, 1868, p. 336.

On this verse, one of the great Hebrew scholars of our day, Dr. Cyrus H. Gordon, has exactly expressed the view of Jews throughout the ages, in saying: "These are great words that make history. Centuries later in the time of Ezra and Nehemiah, people thought that these words were being fulfilled. But history has shown that the Second Commonwealth was not the fulfillment of Amos's prophecy. Yet Amos's immortal words will continue to cry out for fulfillment until every promise comes true. His words are inseparable from the vigor of Israel down to the present time; and his message of hope has encouraged Israel to survive millennia of disaster." Cyrus H. Gordon: "Introduction to Old Testament Times," 1953, p. 215.

2. Among those affirming two different periods of Israel's return, see, e.g., Samuel Hinds Wilkinson: "The Israel Promises and their Fulfillment," London, 1936, pp. 121-129; Ed. Bickersteth: "The Restoration of the Jews to their Own Land," 3rd ed., London, 1852; and many more recent students, e.g., Kellogg, N. West, Pentecost, etc.

3. Keil has a most suggestive comment on this passage—"the gathering of the peoples led by Gog against Israel belongs to the heathen nations living on the borders of the known world ... (and) the boundaries of Israel will also stretch far beyond the limits of Palestine, to the vicinity of these hordes of peoples at the remotest extremities on the north, the east, and the south of our globe." C. F. Keil: *Biblical Commentary on the Prophecies of Ezekiel*, Eng. tr., Vol. II, Edinburgh, pp. 179,180.

4. The comment of Dr. Davidson on this paragraph contains both truth and error. "It may be a question whether there be now any connection between Israel and the land of Canaan. If there be, the condition of restoration to it is faith and obedience on the part of the people. A restoration of Jews still in unbelief to Canaan, even if it should occur, could have no meaning so far as the redemptive providence of God is concerned." A. B. Davidson: "The Book of the Prophet Ezekiel," rev. ed., Cambridge, 1924, p. 287.

5. On a parallel passage, Jeremiah 33:26, a modern commentator is so opposed to any literal interpretation, that he says this is fulfilled in Matthew 19:28, and refers to "special promises to the Twelve who shall rule with Him in heaven." Theo. Laetsch: "Bible Commentary, Jeremiah," St. Louis, Mo., 1952, p. 272.

6. John Calvin: "Commentaries on the Book of the Prophet Jeremiah and the Lamentations,"

Edinburgh, 1854, Vol. IV, p. 207.

Those two great commentators of an earlier era, John Gill (1697-1771) and Adam Clarke (1762-1832) both affirm this chapter teaches the restoration of Israel to Palestine. "The land of Canaan, given to Abraham, etc., shall be again possessed by the Jews their posterity; for without supposing that the Jews upon their call and conversion to their own land, in a literal sense, I see not how we can understand this, and many other prophecies." John Gill: "An Exposition of the Old and New Testament," London, 1810, Vol. I, p. 133. Also Adam Clarke: "The Holy Bible, Containing the Old and New Testaments," London, 1832, pp. 2960-2962.

Chapter 4

1. Nahum Sokolow: "History of Zionism," London, 1919, Vol. II, pp. 179,287.

2. Similar phraseology is found in "The Proclamation of the Rise of the State of Israel," read aloud in Jerusalem by Mr. David Ben Gurion, May 15, 1948. "The Land of Israel was the birthplace of the Jewish people . . . Here they wrote and gave the Bible to the world . . . Impelled by this historic association, Jews strove throughout the centuries to go back to the land of their fathers and regain their statehood."

3. "United Nations Special Committee on Palestine Report to the General Assembly," Vol.

III, Annex A. Lake Success, New York, p. 103.

This love for Zion interpenetrates Jewish literature of every age. Thus Rabbi Hurwitz, writing in 1621, "My beloved children, tell everybody who intends to go to the Holy Land to settle in Jerusalem . . . All good is there, and nothing is lacking . . . The most important point is that it is particularly holy and the gate of heaven. I have much confidence that the Lord will let much knowledge of the Torah spread through me, so that the word may be fulfilled that out of Zion shall go forth the Law (Isaiah 2:3)." From Franz Kobler: "Letters of Jews through the Ages," New York, 1953, Vol. II, p. 484.

4. Philip Doddridge: "Works," Leeds, 1802, Vol. V.

5. Increase Mather: "The Mystery of Israel's Salvation—concerning the Conversion of the Israelitish Nation," London, 1669, pp. 12,53-57 etc.

6. Elhanan Winchester: "A Course of Lectures on the Prophecies that Remain to be Fulfilled," Walpole, 1800, Vol. I, pp. 130-132.

7. Wm. E. Blackstone: "Jesus Is Coming," New York, 1912, p. 236.

8. J. H. Kurtz: "History of the Old Covenant," Eng. tr. Philadelphia, 1859, Vol. I, p. 44.

Among some of the more important volumes discussing affirmatively the restoration of the Jews to Palestine are—John Fry: "Observations on the Unfulfilled Prophecies of Scripture,"

London, 1835; James Bicheno: "The Restoration of Jews, the Crisis of all Nations," London, 1880; Hughes McNeile: "Prophecies relating to the Jewish Nation," London, 1840; Edward Bickersteth: "The Restoration of the Jews to their Own Land," London, 1842; James Allin: "Old Testament Prophecies Relative to the Return and Restoration of the Twelve Tribes to the Land of Palestine," London, 1855. (A learned work of over four hundred pages, now rarely seen.) A good arrangement of most of these prophecies may be found in T. R. Birks: "Outlines of Unfulfilled Prophecy," London, 1854; pp. 263-302. For chapters on the same, see e.g., Joseph A. Seiss: "The Last Times," 6th ed., Philadelphia, 1864, pp. 183-208; William R. Nicholson, in Nathaniel West (ed.), "Premillennial Essays," Chicago, 1879, pp. 220-240; Wilbur M. Smith: "World Crises and Prophetic Scriptures," Chicago, 1952, pp. 180-205; John Wilkinson: "Israel My Glory," rev. ed., London, 1921 (1st ed. 1889) pp. 48-61.

There is a great mass of important material relating to the interpretation of the prophetic Scriptures in the hundreds of articles appearing in the then widely-read prophetic journals of a century ago, such as "Journal of Prophecy," London, 1849-1858; "The Investigator," London, 1831-1836; "The Jewish Expositor and Friend of Israel," London, 1816-1834; "Prophetic News," 1877-   ; "The Morning Watch," Edinburgh, 1888-1895; "Jewish Intelligence and Monthly Account of the Proceedings of the London Society for Promoting Christianity Among the Jews," 1830-1885; "Prophetic Times," 1866 etc. In the issue for November 1866, of the "Prophetic Times" in an article on "The Jews and the Holy Land," I recently read an account of the International Society of the Orient, of Basle, the purpose of which was to obtain certain privileges from Turkey concerning the building up of Palestine—which even Sokolow does not mention. Many of these series are very scarce, and, for this and other reasons, no modern writer on prophecy seem to have even attempted to research them.

Chapter 5

1. Chaim Weizmann, in "The Jewish People in Palestine." Statement made before the Palestine Royal Commission, in Jerusalem, on November 25, 1936. 2nd ed., London, 1939, p. 17.

2. Nahum Sokolow: "Hibbath Zion," Jerusalem, 1935, pp. 69-74, and the same author's monumental work, "History of Zionism," 1600-1918, London, 1919, Vol. I, pp. 179,277.

3. Art. "Zionism," in "Encyclopaedia Britannica," new ed., 1966, Vol. 23, p. 956B. (An excellent article.)

Some statistics regarding population in Palestine might be introduced here. It has been estimated that the population of Palestine during the life of our Lord was between 500,000 and 600,000 and of Jerusalem between 55,000 and 95,000 (T. W. Mansen: "The Servant Messiah," Cambridge Univ. Press, 1953, pp. 10, 11). In 1839 there were not more than 3,000 Jews in Jerusalem, and about 8,000 in all of Palestine. The number of Jews in Palestine in 1880 was 35,000; in 1900 about 70,000; in 1908, 41,000; in 1920, 58,000; in 1922, 83,000; in 1931, 175,000; two years later, 227,-000, two years later, 375,000; and in 1946 it was 675,000. By 1952 it had reached 1,500,000, and by 1965 there were 2,155,000 Jews in Israel. By 1967, the population was 2,635,000.

4. Rufus Learsi: "Fulfillment. The Epic Story of Zionism." Cleveland, 1951, p. 88. (There are slight variations in the translated English texts.)

   "Zionism." London, 1920, p. 31. See the "Historical Connection of the Jewish People with Palestine," Jerusalem, 1946.

   N. Sokolow: "History of Zionism," Vol. I, pp. 268ff. In fairness to Herzl it should be stated that on some later occasions he would make brief references to the Jewish faith, e.g., at the Fourth Zionist Congress, London, 1900, when he said: "Our re-appearance in the land of our fathers, prophesied by Holy Writ, sung by our poets, yearned for midst tears by our stricken nation."

5. For the Balfour Declaration, see Sokolow: "History," Vol. II, pp. 83ff.: Leonard Stein: "The Balfour Declaration," London, 1961. (A work of nearly 700 pages.)

6. Art. "Zionism," in "Encyclopaedia Britannica," new ed. (1966), Vol. 23, p. 956B. With the kind permission of the publishers, "The Encyclopaedia Britannica."

7. Some of the literature produced by this event may here be mentioned: Mrs. Jessie Sage Roberts: "The Deliverance of Jerusalem," New York, 1918; "Jerusalem. Its Redemption and Future. The Great Drama of Deliverance described by Eyewitnesses," New York, 1918. W. T. Massey: "How Jerusalem Was Won," London, 1918. An example of utterly unfounded assertions made at this time is that by A. E. Thompson, then of the American Church in Jerusalem, in a chapter on "The Capture of Jerusalem," in which he refers to this event as "the beginning of the end of all imperialism ... the beginning of the end of the declaration of the Gospel," in "Light on Prophecy," New York, 1918, pp. 144ff.

8. The entire resolution is found most conveniently in the very important publication, "United Nations Resolution on Palestine 1947-1965" Beirut, 1966, pp. 39,40.

9. "Palestine Royal Commission Report." London, 1937, Pt. I, Ch. XXII. "A Plan of Partition", pp. 380-393. For the later plans for partition, which were carried out, see the volume referred to in Note 8, pp. 11-37.

10. On the subject of Israel and the United Nations, the following will be found helpful— "The Jewish Plan for Palestine. Memoranda

and Statements." Presented by the Jewish Agency of Palestine to the United Nations Special Committee on Palestine. Jerusalem, 1947, pp. xiv,559; "Jerusalem and the United Nations," Israel Office of Information, 1953; pp. 27; "Israel and the United Nations." Prepared for the Carnegie Endowment for International Peace. New York, 1956, pp. 332; Jacob Robinson: "Palestine and the United Nations," Washington, D. C. 1947; Paul Mohn: "Jerusalem and the United States," New York, 1950. Sami Hadawi (ed.) "United Nations Resolutions on Palestine," Beirut, Lebanon, 1966. (Contains the Resolutions for the Internationalization of Jerusalem). "United Nations Special Committee on Palestine," Lake Success, New York, 1947. 5 Vols.

For the origin and growth of the modern State of Israel, the following, arranged chronologically, will be found helpful.

Norman Bentwich: "Fulfillment in the Promised Land," London, 1939

Abraham Revusky: "Jews in Palestine," New York, 1945

Barbara W. Tuchman: "Bible and Sword." England and Palestine, from the Bronze Age to Balfour. New York, 1956 (A truly invaluable work).

Jorge Garcia-Granadoz: "The Birth of Israel." "The Drama As I Saw It," New York, 1948

J. C. Hurewitz: "The Struggle for Palestine," London, 1950

Folke Bernadotte: "To Jerusalem," London, 1951

Rufus Learsi: "Fulfillment. The Epic Story of Zionism," Cleveland, 1951

H. Sacher: "Israel: The Establishment of a State," 1952

David Ben Gurion: "Rebirth and Destiny of Israel," New York, 1954

James Parkes: "End of an Exile. Israel, The Jews, and the Gentile World," New York, 1954

Norman Bentwich: "Israel Resurgent," London, 1960

L. F. Rushbrooke Williams: "The State of Israel," 1957

There is an excellent article, "Israel," in the new ed. (1966) of the Encyclopaedia Britannica, Vol. XII, pp. 697-702. For some strange reason, few seem to be aware of an invaluable collection of material, in Julia E. Johnsen: Palestine: "Jewish Homeland," New York 1946 with 40 pages of bibliography.

Chapter 6

1. H. C. Leupold: "Exposition of Genesis." Columbus, Ohio, 1942, p. 504. With the kind permission of the publisher, the Wartburg Press, Columbus, Ohio.

2. Kirkpatrick acknowledges that "History records no one single occasion upon which the nations and tribes mentioned in the Psalms were united

in a confederacy against Israel." The only satis-
factory treatment of the prophetic significance
of this Psalm that I have seen is by the late
Dr. A. C. Gaebelein. "Perhaps present day history may give us a little light. As Palestine is
being resettled by the Jews, having a population of over 300,000, the Arabs make strong
opposition to further aggressions. They are the
Ishmaelites. Perhaps as the restoration programme continues, it may come to such a confederacy as here indicated, and as other nations
are to come upon the scene once more, so
ancient Moab and Ammon, may have a revival,
and reveal their God opposition again. But this
is a mere suggestion. We must wait till God
fulfills His Word." A. C. Gaebelein: "The Book
of Psalms," New York, 1939, p. 320.

3. "The World Almanac for 1965," p. 321. One
cannot help but wonder why this particular
statement has been dropped from the 1967
edition.

4. In the prophecy of Obadiah, verse 16 is somewhat a parallel to the thought of the verses
we have been considering. Pusey is correct in
affirming that "what Edom had done, and what
had befallen Judah, were types of the future
development of the fate of Judah and the attitude of Edom towards it, which go on fulfilling
themselves more and more until the Day of
the Lord upon all nations." See also Amos 1:11.

NOTE: In *Foreign Affairs*, Jan. 1952, (Vol.
30), is a truly profound article by Dr. Charles

H. Malik, President of the General Assembly of the United Nations, 1958-1959, a learned Lebanese, and devout Christian, in which he says—"To dismiss the present conflict between the children of Isaac and the children of Ishmael, who are all children of Abraham, as just another ordinary politico-economic struggle, is to have no sense whatever for the awful and holy and ultimate in history. The rise of Israel presents a great challenge; that of the mystery of the two children of Abraham after the flesh," (p. 245).

Chapter 7

1. J. C. Ryle: "Expository Thoughts on the Gospels, St. Luke," Vol. II, p. 373. Rev. ed., London, 1910.

   I have not felt it was necessary to give bibliographic details for the New Testament commentaries referred to here, as they are all easily available. A lengthy discussion of this passage is found, unexpectedly, in C. F. Keil's comment on Ezekiel 37:15-28, in which he favorably quotes Hengstenberg's error that this means that "Jerusalem will become the possession of the Israel of the Christian church." "Biblical Commentary on the Prophecies of Ezekiel," Vol. II, pp. 155-157.

2. Wilbur M. Smith: "World Crises and the Prophetic Scriptures," Chicago, 1952, p. 235.

Chapter 8

1. H. C. Leupold: "Exposition of Daniel," Columbus, 1949, p. 430. The famous historian Milman has aptly said: "Jerusalem might almost seem to be a place under a peculiar curse; it has probably witnessed a greater portion of human misery than any other spot under the sun."

The most satisfying list I have seen of battles waged in and around this city is in a book by Jacob Gartenhaus, "The Rebirth of a Nation," who has kindly granted me permission to reprint it here.

"B.C.:

1. By David about 1000.
2. Plunder of the Temple and city by Shoshenk I of Egypt about 930 (I Kings 14:25; II Chronicles 12:2).
3. Partial overthrow by Jehoash of Israel about 790 (II Kings 14:13).
4. Attack by Aram and N. Israel about 734
5. Siege by Sennacherib, 701
6. Surrender to Nebuchadnezzar, 597
7. His siege and destruction, 587-6
8. Sack by the Persians, 450
9. Destruction by Ptolemy Sotar, 320
10. Siege of Akra by Antiochus Epiphanes, 198
11. Capture by Jason, 170
12. Destruction by Antiochus Epiphanes, 168
13. Siege of Akra and the Temple, 163-2

14. Siege of Akra, 146
15. Siege and levelling of walls by Antiochus VII, 134
16. Unsuccessful siege by the Nabateans, 65
17. Siege, capture, and destruction by Pompey, 63
18. Sack of Temple by Crassus, 54
19. Capture by Parthians, 40
20. Siege and partial destruction of Herod and Sosius, 37

A.D.:
1. Insurrection and some ruin on the visit of Florus, 65
2. Unsuccessful siege by Cestus Gallus, 66
3. The great siege and destructions by Titus, 70.
4. Seizure by the Jews under Bar Chocheba, 131
5. Capture and devastation by Hadrian, 132
6. Capture and plunder by Chosroes, the Persian, 614
7. Recapture by Heraclius, 628
8. Occupation by Omar, 637
9. Capture by Moslem rebels, 842
10. Ruin of Christian buildings, 937
11. Occupation by the Fatimite Dynasty, 969
12. Destruction by Khalif Hakim, 1010
13. Occupation by the Seljik Turk, 1075
14. Siege and capture by Afdhal, 1096

15. Siege, capture and massacre by Godfrey, 1099
16. Occupation by Saladin, 1187
17. Destruction of walls, 1219
18. Capture by the Emir of Kerak, 1229
19. Surrender to Fredrick II, 1239
20. Capture by the Kharesimians, 1244
21. Plunder by Arabs, 1480
22. Occupation by Turks, 1547
23. Bombardment by Turks, 1825
24. Occupation by Ibrahim Pasha, the Egyptian, 1831
25. Re-occupation by the Turks, 1841
26. Deliverance of Jerusalem by Field Marshall Viscount Allenby, G.C.B., G.C.M.G., December 11, 1917."

(Jacob Gartenhaus: The Rebirth of a Nation, p. 101).

2. C. H. H. Wright: "Zechariah and His Prophecies," 2nd ed., London, 1879, p. 364

3. In discussing this temple, Walter Scott reminds us that "Jerusalem is the only city on earth where a temple of stone is divinely sanctioned," and then adds, "God is not in this movement, which is undertaken for political ends and purposes." Govett strangely contradicts himself here. He first says that the temple mentioned here must refer to a temple in heaven, as in 11:19; 14:17; and 16:17; but then admits that "the temple of Jerusalem will be yet rebuilt by the Jews in unbelief, and be the scene of wickedness greater than has ever appeared."

Robert Govett: "The Apocalypse Expounded by Scripture," London, 1929, pp. 218, 219. As far back as 1835, John Fry in his excellently written work, "Observations in the Unfulfilled Prophecies of Scriptures," commented on this particular coming event. "The first restored Israelites will certainly begin as soon as possible to restore their temple. But this must be a work of time: the probability is, that like the children of the Babylonian captivity, they will first of all erect an altar for the performance of their ceremonies," (p. 47). Such a project has more than once been proposed by the Jews—see Joseph Salvador: "Paris, Rome and Jerusalem"; and Moss Hess: "Rome and Jerusalem," 8th letter. A more recent discussion is in D. M. Panton: "The Panton Papers," New York, 1925, pp. 73-77. On this subject see a most informing article "Jerusalem: A Third Temple," in *Christianity Today.* July 21, 1967, p. 34.

4. Robert Govett: ibid, pp. 246, 247

5. Lenski, Richard C. H.: "Interpretation of Revelation," p. 346.

6. On the new boundaries of Jeremiah 31:38-40, there is a most interesting discussion in George T. B. Davis: "Rebuilding Palestine according to Prophecy." Philadelphia, 1935, pp. 34-38. Calvin again spiritualizes: "The perpetuity of which the prophet speaks is that which corresponds with the character of Christ's kingdom, and is therefore spiritual," p. 152.

7. David Baron: "The Visions and Prophecies of

Zechariah." 3rd ed., London, 1919. p. 494. Calvin, characteristically, makes verses 1-4 refer exclusively to the Church! "Whenever the ungodly prevail, and no hope shines on us, let us remember how often and by what various means God has wonderfully delivered His Church as it were from death," etc. John Calvin: "Commentaries on the Twelve Minor Prophets." Vol. V, p. 410. A contemporary commentator, W. J. Dean, repeats such an unacceptable interpretation, "The literal interpretation must be resigned, and the whole prophecy must be taken to adumbrate the kingdom of God in its trial, development, and triumph. Verse 3 refers to the general course of God's providence in defending His people."

Chapter 9

1. Nathaniel West: "The Thousand Years in Both Testaments," p. 454
2. C. F. Keil: "The Twelve Minor Prophets," Eng. tr. Vol. I, Edinburgh, 1868, p. 72.